序

我只懂一门外文——英文，还不精通。因此轻易不敢做翻译工作，尤其译诗。我虽然也译过一两本国王和总统的诗，那都是"上头"给我的任务，我只好努力而为。至于我自己喜爱、又极愿和读者共同享受而翻译出来的书，只有两本，那就是《先知》和《吉檀迦利》。

1930年母亲逝世之后，我病了一场，病榻无聊，把从前爱读的、黎巴嫩诗人纪伯伦写的散文诗《先知》重读了一遍。纪伯伦从小饱经忧患，到处漂流，最后在美国定居，他用阿拉伯文写了许多作品，已被译成18种不同的文字。以后他又用英文写了许多作品，而这本《先知》被世界各地的读者们称为他的代表作。

我那时觉得有喷溢的欲望，愿意让不会读原文的读者，也能享受我读这本书时的欣悦、景仰和伤感。

《先知》的好处，是作者以纯洁美丽的诗的语言，说出了境界高超、眼光远大、既深奥又平凡的处世为人的道理，译来觉得又容易又顺利，又往往会不由自主地落下眼泪。

我知道我的译文，只能汲取了大海中的一滴，但只此一滴，我也愿贡献给不会读原文的读者们，来分享我译诗时的"辛苦"和享受。

——冰心

前言

纪·哈·纪伯伦是美籍黎巴嫩阿拉伯诗人、作家、画家,于 1883 年生于黎巴嫩山。他 12 岁时到过美国,两年后又回到东方,进入贝鲁特的阿希马大学。1903 年,他再次到美国,待了 5 年,多居住在波士顿。之后他到巴黎学画,同时漫游欧洲;1912 年回到纽约,在那里居住。

纪伯伦的一生,短暂而辉煌,经受了颠沛流离、贫病交迫、爱情波折、失去亲人等苦痛。这些苦难,没有将他打倒,他将残酷的现实当做圣殿,把爱与美作为信仰,深情地为生命献上一首首美妙的歌曲。当他感到死神将临时,为了让生命之火燃烧得更加光耀,他忘记了身上的病痛,终日伏案创作。在生命的最后岁月,他写下了传遍阿拉伯的诗篇《朦胧中的祖国》,他讴歌道:"您在我们的灵魂中——是火,是光;您在我的胸膛里——是我悸动的心脏。"

纪伯伦被称为"艺术天才""黎巴嫩文坛骄子",是阿拉伯现代小说、艺术和散文的重要奠基人。他的青年时代以小说创作为主,作品几乎都是用阿拉伯语写成,定居美国后逐渐转为以写散文诗为主,先后使用阿拉伯语和英语创作。他的作品蕴含了丰富的社会性和东方精神,抒发了丰富而强烈的情感。在巴黎艺术学院学习绘画期间,罗丹曾经肯定地评价纪伯伦说:"这个阿拉伯青年将成为伟大的艺术家。"

他的主要作品有《泪与笑》《先知》《沙与沫》等,《先知》是他最受欢迎的作品。目前,他的作品已经被译成多国文字出版发行。纪伯伦同鲁迅、泰戈尔一样,是近代东方文学走向世界的先驱,是"站在东西方文化桥梁上的巨人"。同时,以他为中坚形成的阿拉伯第一个文学流派——叙美派全球闻名。

世间所有相遇，都是久别重逢
——纪伯伦散文诗选

【黎巴嫩】纪伯伦 著　冰心 等 译

江苏凤凰科学技术出版社·南京

图书在版编目（CIP）数据

世间所有相遇，都是久别重逢：纪伯伦散文诗选：汉英对照 /（黎巴嫩）纪伯伦著；冰心等译 . — 南京：江苏凤凰科学技术出版社, 2015.11（2022.5 重印）
（易人外语）
ISBN 978-7-5537-5474-1

Ⅰ.①世… Ⅱ.①纪…②冰… Ⅲ.①英语 – 阅读教学 – 自学参考资料②散文诗 – 作品集 – 黎巴嫩 – 现代 ① H319.4：Ⅰ

中国版本图书馆 CIP 数据核字 (2015) 第 230816 号

易人外语
世间所有相遇，都是久别重逢——纪伯伦散文诗选

著　　者	【黎巴嫩】纪伯伦
译　　者	冰　心 等
责 任 编 辑	祝　萍
责 任 监 制	方　晨
出 版 发 行	江苏凤凰科学技术出版社
出版社地址	南京市湖南路 1 号 A 楼，邮编：210009
出版社网址	http://www.pspress.cn
印　　刷	天津丰富彩艺印刷有限公司
开　　本	880 mm × 1 230 mm　1/32
印　　张	10
字　　数	150 000
版　　次	2015 年 11 月第 1 版
印　　次	2022 年 5 月第 5 次印刷
标 准 书 号	ISBN 978-7-5537-5474-1
定　　价	45.00 元

图书如有印装质量问题，可随时向我社印务部调换。

故乡奇崛秀美的景色，为他的艺术创作插上了翅膀。纪伯伦的作品大多以"爱"和"美"为主题，通过大胆的想象与象征的表现手法，来表达深沉的情感与远大的理想。他曾说："整个地球都是我的祖国，全部人类都是我的乡亲。"他的许多作品都带有基督教色彩，经常流露出愤世嫉俗的态度或者表现某种神秘的力量。

1927年，冰心先生在美国朋友处读到纪伯伦的《先知》，并被它深深打动。她说："那满含东方气息的超妙的哲理和流丽的文字，予我以极深的印象。"1931年，冰心先生将他的《先知》翻译成中文。从20世纪50年代起，纪伯伦的作品开始被越来越多的中国读者所了解。近几十年来，我国又陆续出版了一些纪伯伦的作品。这位黎巴嫩的文坛骄子，在中国有了越来越多的知音。

目录

第一卷 爱·美

先知 / 8
On Love/ 爱 8
On Marriage/ 婚姻 13
On Children/ 孩子 15
On Giving/ 施与 18
On Friendship/ 友谊 24
On Beauty/ 美 27

泪与笑 / 32
Laughter and Tears/ 笑与泪 32
Before the Throne of Beauty/ 在美神的宝座前 37

沙与沫 / 42

第二卷 生·死

先知 / 64
On Work/ 工作 64
On Buying and Selling/ 买卖 70
On Teaching/ 教授 73
On Talking/ 谈话 76
On Death/ 死 79
On Time/ 时光 82

泪与笑 / 86
The City of the Dead/ 逝者之城 86
A Poet's Death Is His Life/ 诗人的死就是生 91

沙与沫 / 96

第三卷　魂·物

先知 / 126
On Religion/ 宗教 126
On Self-Knowledge/ 自知 131
On Prayer/ 祈祷 133
On Eating and Drinking/ 饮食 138
On Houses/ 居室 141
On Clothes/ 衣服 147

泪与笑 / 150
Vision/ 梦 150
Song of the Wave/ 浪之歌 153
The Creation/ 造物 157
Song of the Rain/ 雨之歌 160
Song of the Flower/ 花之歌 164

沙与沫 / 168

第四卷　哀·乐

先知 / 188
On Pain/ 苦痛 188
On Pleasure/ 逸乐 191
On Joy and Sorrow/ 哀乐 198

泪与笑 / 200
Yesterday and Today/ 今与昔 200

沙与沫 / 208

第五卷　是·非

先知 / 252
On Good and Evil/ 善恶 252
On Crime and Punishment/ 罪与罚 257
On Freedom/ 自由 266
On Laws/ 法律 272
The Farewell/ 言别 276

泪与笑 / 300
The Criminal/ 罪犯 300
Leave Me, My Blamer/ 致非难者 303

沙与沫 / 310

第一卷
爱·美

先知 （冰心 译）

On Love

Then said Almitra, "Speak to us of Love."

And he raised his head and looked upon the people, and there fell a stillness[1] upon them. And with a great voice he said:

When love beckons to you, follow him, though his ways are hard and steep.

And when his wings enfold[2] you yield to him, though the sword hidden among his pinions may wound you.

And when he speaks to you believe in him, though his voice may shatter your dreams as the north wind lays waste the garden.

For even as love crowns you so shall he crucify[3] you. Even as he is for your growth so is he for your pruning.

Even as he ascends to your height and caresses your tenderest branches that quiver in the sun, so shall he descend to your roots and shake them in their clinging to the earth.

Like sheaves of corn he gathers you unto himself.

He threshes you to make you naked.

He sifts you to free you from your husks.

He grinds you to whiteness.

He kneads you until you are pliant;

And then he assigns you to his sacred fire, that you may become sacred bredad for God's sacred feast.

All these things shall love do unto you that you may know the secrets of your heart, and in that knowledge become a fragment of Life's heart.

But if in your fear you would seek only love's peace and love's pleasure,

Then it is better for you that you cover your nakedness and pass out of love's threshing-floor,

Into the seasonless world where you shall laugh, but not all of your laughter, and weep, but not all of your tears.

Love gives naught but itself and takes naught but from itself.

Love possesses not nor would it be possessed;

For love is sufficient unto love.

When you love you should not say, "God is in my heart," but rather, "I am in the heart of God."

And think not you can direct the course of love, for love, if it finds you worthy, directs your course.

Love has no other desire but to fulfill itself.

But if you love and must needs have desires, let these be your desires:

To melt and be like a running[4] brook that sings its melody to the night.

To know the pain of too much tenderness.

To be wounded by your own understanding of love,

And to bleed willingly and joyfully.

To wake at dawn with a winged heart and give thanks for another day of loving;

To rest at the noon hour and meditate love's ecstasy;

To return home at eventide with gratitude;

And then to sleep with a prayer for the beloved in your heart and a song of praise upon your lips.

热词天地

1.stillness ['stɪlnəs] *n.* 静止；沉静
2.enfold [ɪn'fəʊld] *vt.* 拥抱；包裹；折叠；围绕
3.crucify ['kru:sɪfaɪ] *vt.* 折磨；十字架上钉死；克制
4.running ['rʌnɪŋ] *n.* 运转；赛跑；流出 *adj.* 连续的；流动的；跑着的；运转着的
  lay waste 损毁；荒废
  sacred fire 圣火；真挚的爱；天才

爱

于是爱尔美差说:"请给我们谈爱。"
他举头望着民众,他们一时静默了。他用洪亮的声音说:

当爱向你们召唤的时候,跟随着他,
虽然他的路程艰险而陡峻。
当他的翅翼围卷你们的时候,屈服于他,
虽然那藏在羽翮中间的剑刃许会伤毁你们。
当他对你们说话的时候,信从他,
虽然他的声音也许会把你们的梦魂击碎,如同北风吹荒了林园。

爱虽给你加冠,他也要将你钉在十字架上。他虽栽培你,他也刈剪你。
他虽升到你的最高处,抚惜你在日中颤动的枝叶,
他也要降到你的根下,摇动你的根柢的一切关节,使之归土。
如同一捆稻粟,他把你束聚起来。
他舂打你使你赤裸。
他筛分你使你脱壳。
他磨碾你直至洁白。
他揉搓你直至柔韧。
然后他送你到他的圣火上去,使你成为上帝圣筵上的圣饼。
这些都是爱要给你们做的事情,使你知道自己心中的秘密,在这知识中你便成了"生命"心中的一屑。

假如你在你的疑惧中,只寻求爱的和平与逸乐,
那不如掩盖你的裸露,而躲过爱的筛打,而走入那没有季候的世界,在那里你将欢笑,却不是尽量地笑悦;你将哭泣,却没有流干了眼泪。

爱除自身外无施与，除自身外无接受。
爱不占有，也不被占有。
因为爱在爱中满足了。
当你爱的时候，你不要说，"上帝在我的心中"，却要说"我在上帝的心里"。
不要想你能导引爱的路程，因为若是他觉得你配，他就导引你。
爱没有别的愿望，只要成全自己。

但若是你爱，而且需求愿望，就让以下的做你的愿望吧：
溶化了你自己，像溪流般对清夜吟唱着歌曲。
要知道过度温存的痛苦。
让你对爱的了解毁伤了你自己，
而且甘愿地喜乐地流血。

清晨醒起，以喜蜕的心来致谢这爱的又一日；
日中静息，默念爱的浓欢；
晚潮退时，感谢地回家；
然后在睡时祈祷，因为有被爱者在你的心中，有赞美之歌在你的唇上。

On Marriage

Then Almitra spoke again and said, "And what of Marriage, master?"

And he answered saying:

You were born together, and together you shall be forevermore.

You shall be together when the white wings of death scatter your days.

Ay, you shall be together even in the silent memory of God.

But let there be spaces in your togetherness[1],

And let the winds of the heavens dance between you,

Love one another, but make not a bond of love:

Let it rather be a moving sea between the shores of your souls.

Fill each other's cup but drink not from one cup.

Give one another of your bread but eat not from the same loaf.

Sing and dance together and be joyous, but let each one of you be alone,

Even as the strings of a lute are alone though they quiver with the same music.

Give your hearts, but not into each other's keeping.

For only the hand of Life can contain your hearts.

And stand together, yet not too near together,

For the pillars of the temple stand apart,

And the oak tree and the cypress grow not in each other's shadow.

热词天地

1.togetherness [tə'geðənəs] *n.* 相聚，家庭聚会；团结精神；归属感

婚姻

爱尔美差又说:"夫子,婚姻怎样讲呢?"
他回答说:
你们一块儿出世,也要永远合一。
在死的白翼隔绝你们的岁月的时候,你们也要合一。
噫,连在静默地忆想上帝之时,你们也要合一。
不过在你们合一之中,要有间隙。
让天风在你们中间舞荡。

彼此相爱,但不要做成爱的系链:
只让他在你们灵魂的沙岸中间,做一个流动的海。
彼此斟满了杯,却不要在同一杯中啜饮。
彼此递赠着面包,却不要在同一块上取食。
快乐地在一处舞唱,却仍让彼此静独,
连琴上的那些弦也是单独的,虽然他们在同一的音调中颤动。

彼此赠献你们的心,却不要互相保留。
因为只有"生命"的手,才能把持你们的心。
要站在一处,却不要太密迩:
因为殿里的柱子,也是分立在两旁,
橡树和松柏,也不在彼此的荫中生长。

On Children

And a woman who held a babe against her bosom said, "Speak to us of Children."
And he said:

Your children are not your children.
They are the sons and daughters of Life's longing for itself.
They come through you but not from you,
And though they are with you, yet they belong not to you.

You may give them your love but not your thoughts.
For they have their own thoughts.
You may house their bodies but not their souls,
For their souls dwell[1] in the house of tomorrow, which you cannot visit, not even in your dreams.

You may strive[2] to be like them, but seek not to make them like you.
For life goes not backward nor tarries with yesterday.

You are the bows from which your children as living arrows are sent forth[3].

The archer sees the mark upon the path of the infinite, and He bends you with His might[4] that His arrows may go swift and far.

Let your bending in the archer's hand be for gladness;

For even as He loves the arrow that flies, so He loves also the bow that is stable.

热词天地

1.dwell [dwel] *vi.* 居住；存在于；细想某事
2.strive [straɪv] *vi.* 努力；奋斗；抗争
3.forth [fɔːθ] *adv.* 向前，向外
4.might [maɪt] *n.* 力量；威力；势力
   held a babe against her bosom 怀里抱着孩子
   belong (not) to （不）属于

孩子

于是一个怀中抱着孩子的妇人说:"请给我们谈孩子。"
他说:

你们的孩子,都不是你们的孩子。
乃是"生命"为自己所渴望的儿女。
他们是凭借你们而来,却不是从你们而来,
他们虽和你们同在,却不属于你们。

你们可以给他们以爱,却不可给他们以思想。
因为他们有自己的思想。
你们可以荫庇他们的身体,却不能荫庇他们的灵魂。
因为他们的灵魂,是住在"明日"的宅中,那是你们在梦中也不能想见的。
你们可以努力去模仿他们,却不能使他们来像你们。
因为生命是不倒行的,也不与"昨日"一同停留。

你们是弓,你们的孩子是从弦上发出的生命的箭矢。
那射者在无穷之中看定了目标,也用神力将你们引满,使他的箭矢迅速而遥远地射了出去。
让你们在射者手中的"弯曲",成为喜乐罢;
因为他爱那飞出的箭,也爱那静止的弓。

On Giving

Then said a rich man, "Speak to us of Giving."
And he answered:

You give but little when you give of your possessions.
It is when you give of yourself that you truly give.
For what are your possessions but things you keep and guard for fear you may need them tomorrow?
And tomorrow, what shall tomorrow bring to the over-prudent dog burying bones in the trackless[1] sand as he follows the pilgrims to the holy city?
And what is fear of need but need itself?
Is not dread[2] of thirst when your well is full, the thirst that is unquenchable?

There are those who give little of the much which they have—and they give it for recognition and their hidden desire makes their gifts unwholesome.

And there are those who have little and give it all.

These are the believers in life and the bounty[3] of life, and their coffer is never empty.

There are those who give with joy, and that joy is their reward.

And there are those who give with pain, and that pain is their baptism[4].

And there are those who give and know not pain in giving, nor do they seek joy, nor give with mindfulness of virtue;

They give as in yonder valley the myrtle breathes its fragrance into space.

Through the hands of such as these God speaks, and from behind their eyes He smiles upon the earth.

It is well to give when asked, but it is better to give unasked, through understanding;

And to the open-handed the search for one who shall receive is joy greater than giving.

And is there aught you would withhold?

All you have shall some day be given;

Therefore give now, that the season of giving may be yours and not your inheritors'.

You often say, "I would give, but only to the deserving."

The trees in your orchard say not so, nor the flocks in your pasture.

They give that they may live, for to withhold is to perish.

Surely he who is worthy to receive his days and his nights is worthy of all else from you.

And he who has deserved to drink from the ocean of life deserves to fill his cup from your little stream.

And what desert greater shall there be than that which lies in the courage and the confidence, nay the charity, of receiving?

And who are you that men should rend their bosom and unveil their pride, that you may see their worth naked and their pride unabashed?

See first that you yourself deserve to be a giver, and an instrument of giving.

For in truth it is life that gives unto life while you, who deem yourself a giver, are but a witness.

And you receivers...and you are all receivers...assume no weight of gratitude, lest you lay a yoke upon yourself and upon him who gives.

Rather rise together with the giver on his gifts as on wings;

For to be overmindful of your debt, is to doubt his generosity who has the freehearted earth for mother, and God for father.

热词天地

1. trackless ['træklɪs] *adj.* 无足迹的，无路的，不在轨道上行驶的
2. dread [dred] *n.* 恐惧，畏惧；令人恐惧的事物
3. bounty ['baʊntɪ] *n.* （由政府提供的）奖金，赏金；慷慨，大方；赠物，赠金
4. baptism ['bæptɪzəm] *n.* （基督教的）洗礼；严峻考验

施与

于是一个富人说:"请给我们谈施与。"
他回答说:

你把你的产业给人,那只算给了一点。
当你以身布施的时候,那才是真正的施与。
因为你的财产,岂不是你保留着的恐怕"明日"或许需要它们的东西么?
但是"明日",那只过虑的犬,随着香客上圣城去,却把骨头埋在无痕迹的沙土里,"明日"能把什么给他呢?
除了需要的本身之外,需要还忧惧什么呢?
当你在井泉充溢的时候愁渴,那你的渴不是更难解么?

有人有许多财产,却只把一小部分给人——他们为求名而施与,那潜藏的欲念,使他们的礼物不完美。
有人只有一点财产,却全部都给人。
这些人相信生命和生命的丰富,他们的宝柜总不空虚。

有人喜乐地施与,那喜乐就是他们的酬报。
有人痛苦地施与,那痛苦就是他们的洗礼。

也有人施与了,而不觉出施与的痛苦,也不寻求快乐,也不有心为善;
他们的施与,如同那边山谷里的桂花,香气在空际浮动。
从这些人的手中,上帝在说话;在他们的眼后,上帝在俯对大地微笑。

因请求而施与的,固然是好,而未受请求,只因默喻而施与的,是更好了;
对于乐善好施的人,去寻求需要他帮助的人的快乐,比施与的快乐还大。

有什么东西你必须保留的呢?

必有一天,你的一切都要交付出来;

趁现在施与罢,这施与的时机是你自己的,而不是你的后人的。

你常说:"我要施与,却只舍给那些配受施与者。"

你果园里的树木和牧场上的羊群,却不这样说。

他们为要生存而施与,因为保留就是毁灭。

凡是配接受白日和黑夜的人们,都配接受你施与的一切。

凡配在生命的海洋里啜饮的,都配在你的小泉里舀满他的杯。

还有什么德行比接受的勇气、信心和善意还大呢?

有谁能使人把他们的心怀敞露,把他们的狷傲揭开,使你能看出他们赤裸的价值和无惭的骄傲?

先省察你自己是否配做一个施与者,是否配做一个施与的器皿。

因为实在说,那只是生命给予生命——你以为自己是施主,其实也不过是一个证人。

你们这些接受者——你们都是接受者——不要负起报恩的重担,恐怕你要把轭加在你自己和施者的身上。

不如和施者在礼物上一齐展翅飞腾;

因为过于思量你们的欠负,就是怀疑了那以慈悲的大地为母、以上帝为父的人的仁心。

On Friendship

And a youth said, "Speak to us of Friendship."
And he answered, saying:
Your friend is your needs answered.
He is your field which you sow with love and reap with thanksgiving.
And he is your board[1] and your fireside.
For you come to him with your hunger, and you seek him for peace.

When your friend speaks his mind you fear not the "nay" in your own mind, nor do you withhold the "ay."
And when he is silent your heart ceases not to listen to his heart;
For without words, in friendship, all thoughts, all desires, all expectations are born and shared, with joy that is unacclaimed[2].
When you part from your friend, you grieve not;

For that which you love most in him may be clearer in his absence, as³ the mountain to the climber is clearer from the plain.

And let there be no purpose in friendship save the deepening of the spirit.

For love that seeks aught⁴ the disclosure of its own mystery is not love but a net cast forth: and only the unprofitable is caught.

And let your best be for your friend.

If he must know the ebb of your tide, let him know its flood also.

For what is your friend that you should seek him with hours to kill?

Seek him always with hours to live.

For it is his to fill your need, but not your emptiness.

And in the sweetness of friendship let there be laughter, and sharing of pleasures.

For in the dew of little things the heart finds its morning and is refreshed.

热词天地

1. board [bɔːd] *n.* 董事会；木板；甲板；膳食
2. acclaim [əˈkleɪm] *vt.* 称赞；赞扬；向……欢呼；向……喝彩
3. as [əz] *conj.* 因为；随着；虽然；依照；当……时 *prep.* 如同；以……的身份
4. aught [ɔːt] *n.* 任何事物（等于 anything）；无物

   part from 向……告别

友谊

于是一个青年说:"请给我们谈友谊。"
他回答说:
你的朋友是你的有回答的需求。
他是你用爱播种、用感谢收获的田地。
他是你的饮食,也是你的火炉。
因为你饥渴地奔向他,你向他寻求平安。

当你的朋友向你倾吐胸臆的时候,你不要怕说出心中的"否",也不要瞒住你心中的"可"。
当他静默的时候,你的心仍要倾听他的心;
因为在友谊里,不用言语,一切的思想,一切的愿望,一切的希冀,都在无声的欢乐中发生而共享了。
当你与朋友别离的时候,不要忧伤;
因为你感到他的最可爱之点,当他不在时愈见清晰,正如登山者从平原上望山峰,也加倍地分明。
愿除了寻求心灵的加深之外,友谊没有别的目的。
因为那只寻求着要泄露自身的神秘的爱,不算是爱,只算是一个撒下的网,只网住一些无益的东西。
让你的最美好的事物,都给你的朋友。
假如他必须知道你潮水的退落,也让他知道你潮水的高涨。
你找他只为消磨光阴的人,还能算是你的朋友么?
你要在生长的时间中去找他。
因为他的时间是满足你的需要,不是填满你的空腹。

在友谊的温柔中,要有欢笑和共同的喜悦。
因为在那微末事物的甘露中,你的心能找到他的清晓而焕发了精神。

On Beauty

And a poet said, "Speak to us of Beauty."
And he answered:

Where shall you seek beauty, and how shall you find her unless she herself be your way and your guide?

And how shall you speak of her except she be the weaver of your speech?

The aggrieved[1] and the injured say, "Beauty is kind and gentle.
Like a young mother half-shy of her own glory she walks among us."
And the passionate say, "Nay, beauty is a thing of might and dread.
Like the tempest[2] he shakes the earth beneath us and the sky above us."

The tired and the weary say, "Beauty is of soft whisperings. She speaks in our spirit.

Her voice yields to our silences like a faint light that quivers in fear of the shadow."

But the restless say, "We have heard her shouting among the mountains,

And with her cries came the sound of hoofs, and the beating of wings and the roaring of lions."

At night the watchmen of the city say, "Beauty shall rise with the dawn from the east."

And at noontide the toilers and the wayfarers say, "We have seen her leaning over the earth from the windows of the sunset."

In winter say the snow-bound, "She shall come with the spring leaping upon the hills."

And in the summer heat the reapers say, "We have seen her dancing with the autumn leaves,and we saw a drift of snow in her hair."

All these things have you said of beauty.
Yet in truth you spoke not of her but of needs unsatisfied,
And beauty is not a need but an ecstasy[3].
It is not a mouth thirsting nor an empty hand stretched forth,
But rather a heart enflamed and a soul enchanted.
It is not the image you would see nor the song you would hear,
But rather an image you see though you close your eyes and a song you hear though you shut your ears.
It is not the sap within the furrowed bark, nor a wing attached to a claw,
But rather a garden for ever in bloom and a flock of angels for ever in flight.

People of Orphalese, beauty is life when life unveils her holy face.
But you are life and you are the veil[4].
Beauty is eternity[5] gazing at itself in a mirror.
But you are eternity and you are the mirror.

热词天地

1.aggrieved [ə'gri:vd] *adj.* 受委屈的，愤愤不平的；权利受到不法侵害的
2.tempest ['tempɪst] *n.* 暴风雨；骚动；动乱
3.ecstasy ['ekstəsɪ] *n.* 狂喜；入迷；忘形
4.veil [veɪl] *n.* 面纱；面罩 *vt.* 以面纱遮掩 *vi.* 蒙上面纱；出现轻度灰雾
5.eternity [ɪ'tɜ:nətɪ] *n.* 来世，来生；不朽；永世

美

于是一个诗人说:"请给我们谈美。"
他回答说:

你们到处追求美,除了她自己做了你的道路,引导着你之外,你如何能找到她呢?
除了她做了你的言语的编造者之外,你如何能谈论她呢?

冤抑的、受伤的人说:"美是仁爱的,柔和的,
如同一位年轻的母亲,在她自己的光荣中半含着羞涩,在我们中间行走。"
热情的人说:"不,美是一种全能的可畏的东西,
暴风似地,撼摇了上天下地。"
疲乏的、忧苦的人说:"美是温柔的微语,在我们心灵中说话。

她的声音传达到我们的寂静中,如同微晕的光,在阴影的恐惧中颤动。"

烦躁的人却说:"我们听见她在万山中叫号,

与她的呼声俱来的,有兽蹄之声,振翼之音,与狮子之吼。"

在夜里守城的人说:"美要与晓暾从东方一同升起。"

在日中的时候,工人和旅客说:"我们曾见她凭倚在落日的窗户上俯视大地。"

在冬日,阻雪的人说:"她要和春天一同来临,跳跃于山峰之上。"

在夏日的炎热里,刈者说:"我们曾看见她与秋叶一同跳舞,我们也看见她的发中有一堆白雪。"

这些都是他们关于美的谈说。

实际上,你却不是谈她,只是谈着你那未曾满足的需要,

美不是一种需要,只是一种欢乐。

她不是干渴的口,也不是伸出的空虚的手,

却是发焰的心,陶醉的灵魂。

她不是那你能看到的形象,能听到的歌声,

却是你虽闭目时也能看见的形象,虽掩耳时也能听见的歌声。

她不是犁痕下树皮中的液汁,也不是在兽爪间垂死的禽鸟,

却是一座永远开花的花园,一群永远飞翔的天使。

阿法利斯的民众呵,在生命揭露圣洁的面容的时候的美,就是生命。

但你就是生命,你也是面纱。

美是永生揽镜自照。

但你就是永生,你也是镜子。

泪与笑

Laughter and Tears

As the Sun withdrew his rays from the garden, and the moon threw cushioned beams upon the flowers, I sat under the trees pondering upon the phenomena[1] of the atmosphere, looking through the branches at the strewn[2] stars which glittered like chips of silver upon a blue carpet; and I could hear from a distance the agitated murmur of the rivulet singing its way briskly into the valley.

When the birds took shelter among the boughs, and the flowers folded their petals, and tremendous silence descended, I heard a rustle of feet through the grass. I took heed and saw a young couple approaching my arbor. They say under a tree where I could see them without being seen.

After he looked about in every direction, I heard the young man saying, "Sit by me, my beloved, and listen to my heart; smile, for your happiness is a symbol of our future; be merry, for the sparkling days rejoice with us.

"My soul is warning me of the doubt in your heart, for doubt in love is a sin." Soon you will be the owner of this vast land, lighted by this beautiful moon; soon you will be the mistress of my palace, and all the servants and maids will obey your commands.

"Smile, my beloved, like the gold smiles from my father's coffers[3].

"My heart refuses to deny you its secret. Twelve months of comfort and travel await us; for a year we will spend my father's gold at the blue lakes of Switzerland, and viewing the edifices of Italy and Egypt, and resting under the Holy Cedars of Lebanon; you will meet the princesses who will envy you for your jewels and clothes.

"All these things I will do for you; will you be satisfied?"

In a little while I saw them walking and stepping on flowers as the rich step upon the hearts of the poor. As they disappeared from my sight, I commenced[4] to make comparison between love and money, and to analyze their position in the heart.

Money! The source of insincere love; the spring of false light and fortune; the well of poisoned water; the desperation of old age!

I was still wandering in the vast desert of contemplation when a forlorn and specter-like couple passed by me and sat on the grass; a young man and a young woman who had left their farming shacks in the nearby fields for this cool and solitary place.

After a few moments of complete silence, I heard the following words uttered with sighs from weather-bitten lips, "Shed not tears, my beloved; love that opens our eyes and enslaves[5] our hearts can give us the blessing of patience. Be consoled in our delay our delay, for we have taken an oath and entered Love's shrine; for our love will ever grow in adversity; for it is in Love's name that we are suffering the obstacles of poverty and the sharpness of misery and the emptiness of separation. I shall attack these hardships until I triumph and place in your hands a strength that will help over all things to complete the journey of life.

"Love—which is God—will consider our sighs and tears as incense[6] burned at His altar and He will reward us with fortitude. Good-bye, my beloved; I must leave before the heartening moon vanishes."

A pure voice, combined of the consuming flame of love, and the hopeless bitterness of longing and the resolved sweetness of patience, said, "Good-bye, my beloved."

They separated, and the elegy to their union was smothered by the wails of my crying heart.

I looked upon slumbering Nature, and with deep reflection discovered the reality of a vast and infinite thing—something no power could demand, influence acquire, nor riches purchase. Nor could it be effaced by the tears of time or deadened by sorrow; a thing which cannot be discovered by the blue lakes of Switzerland or the beautiful edifices of Italy.

It is something that gathers strength with patience, grows despite obstacles, warms in winter, flourishes in spring, casts a breeze in summer, and bears fruit in autumn—I found Love.

热词天地

1. phenomena [fə'nɒmɪnə] *n.* 现象（phenomenon 的复数）
2. strewn [struːn] *adj.* 撒满的；散播的
3. coffers ['kɒfəz] *n.* 金库（coffer 的复数）
4. commence [kə'mens] *vt.* 开始；着手
5. enslave [ɪn'sleɪv] *vt.* 束缚；征服；使某人成为奴隶
6. incense ['ɪnsens] *vt.* 向……焚香；使……发怒　*n.* 香；奉承　*vi.* 焚香

笑与泪

当太阳从花园渐渐收敛余晖,月光在花朵上洒下柔美银光时,我坐在树丛下,凝思着这瞬息万变的天空。透过枝叶,我仰望满天繁星,它们像撒落在蓝色地毯上的银币一样闪闪发亮;我侧耳静听,远处传来山涧的水声。

夜鸟归林,花瓣聚拢,周围一派宁静。我听到急切的脚步声穿过草坪。我留心一看,只见一对青年男女向我的凉棚走来。他们坐在一棵树下,看不见我,我却能看清他俩。

小伙子先四下望了望,然后才听见他说:"坐我身旁吧,我的爱,聆听我的心跳;微笑吧,你的快乐就是我们的未来;高兴起来吧,这些鲜亮的日子都为我们开心。

"我仿佛感觉你的心中仍有疑虑,而对于爱情,怀疑是一种罪责。不久,这片月光下的广阔之地都将属于你;不久,你将是我宫殿的女主人,所有的随从和女仆都将遵从你的旨意。

"微笑吧,亲爱的,像我父亲宝库中的金子般微笑吧。

"我的心执意要在你面前吐露真实秘密。在未来的一年中,我们将共享舒适,携手游玩;在这一年,我们将带上父亲的金钱,到瑞士的蔚蓝湖畔度假;

到意大利的公园，到埃及的古老金字塔游览，在黎巴嫩的神圣雪松下小憩。你遇见的公主都会妒忌你周身的珠光和绫罗。

"这一切都是我要为你准备的，你可满意？"

过了一会儿，我看到他俩慢慢地走着，踩踏着鲜花，恍若富人之足践踏着穷人之心。当他们消失在我的视野，我开始比较爱情与金钱，并分析它们在心灵中所占的地位。

金钱！这虚假爱情的缘由；这伪造的光亮和财富的源泉；这口井满是毒水；这旧时代的绝望！

浮想联翩间，一对情侣如幽灵似的经过我面前，然后坐在不远的草地上；这又是一对青年男女，他们离开田间农舍，来到这个凉爽清寂的地方。

先是一阵彻底的沉默，接下来听到的话语伴随着深深叹息，这话语出自那位口唇干裂的青年："拭去泪水，亲爱的，爱情使我们眼亮心明，让我们成为它的奴仆，也赋予我们坚毅的品性。虽然要推迟婚期，但不要悲伤，因为我们曾盟誓，踏入爱的神殿；我们的爱会在逆境中茁壮成长；因为我们是以爱之名承受着贫穷的羁绊，苦难的折磨和分离的空虚。我一定要击败这些艰辛，直到取得胜利，获得一笔财富献在你的手心，以帮助我们克服生命旅途中的种种艰辛。

爱也就是主，会将我们的悲叹和泪水视作他祭坛上的香火。他也会以坚忍不拔的精神奖赏我们。亲爱的，再见了，在月亮落下之前，我必须走了！"

随后，我听到一阵柔声细语，夹杂着炽烈爱火、无比苦涩的渴望和坚决甜蜜的耐心，那个女孩说："再见吧，我亲爱的！"

之后，他们分了手，为他们奏起的重逢挽歌被我内心的哭喊重重覆盖。

我注视着沉睡的大自然，细细观察，之后发现了一些浩瀚而永恒的东西——一种权力无法强行使之改变、金钱无法买到的东西；一种时间不能抹除，悲伤无法冲淡的东西；一种不能为严冬的悲愁所扼杀的东西；一种在瑞士的蔚蓝湖畔、意大利的游览胜地所找不到的东西。

它集聚力量与耐心，突破障碍成长，在严冬释放暖意，在春天开花遍地，在夏天里送来清风，在秋天繁茂结果——我发现了爱情。

Before the Throne of Beauty

One heavy day I ran away from the grim face of society and the dizzying clamor[1] of the city and directed my weary step to the spacious alley. I pursued the beckoning course of the rivulet and the musical sounds of the birds until I reached a lonely spot where the flowing branches of the trees prevented the sun from the touching the earth.

I stood there, and it was entertaining[2] to my soul—my thirsty soul who had seen naught but the mirage of life instead of its sweetness.

I was engrossed deeply in thought and my spirits were sailing the firmament when a hour, wearing a sprig of grapevine that covered part of her naked body, and a wreath of poppies about her golden hair, suddenly appeared to me. As she realized my astonishment, she greeted me saying, "Fear me not; I am the Nymph of the Jungle."

"How can beauty like yours be committed to live in this place? Please tell mc who your are, and whence you come?" I asked. She sat gracefully on the green grass and responded, "I am the symbol of Nature! I am the ever virgin your forefathers worshipped, and to my honor they erected shrines and temples at Baalbek and Jbeil." And I dared say, "But those temples and shrines were laid waste and the bones of my adoring ancestors became a part of the earth; nothing was left to commemorate[3] their goddess save a pitiful few and the forgotten pages in the book of history."

She replied, "Some goddesses live in the lives of their worshippers and die in their deaths, while some live an eternal[4] and infinite life. My

life is sustained by the world of beauty which you will see where ever you rest your eyes, and this beauty is Nature itself; it is the beginning of the shepherds joy among the hills, and a villagers happiness in the fields, and the pleasure of the awe filled tribes between the mountains and the plains. This Beauty promotes the wise into the throne the truth."

Then I said, "Beauty is a terrible power!" And she retorted, "Human beings fear all things, even yourselves. You fear heaven, the source of spiritual peace; you fear Nature, the haven of rest and tranquility; you fear the God of goodness and accuse him of anger, while he is full of love and mercy."

After a deep silence, mingled with sweet dreams, I asked, "Speak to me of that beauty which the people interpret and define, each one according to his own conception; I have seen her honored and worshipped in different ways and manners."

She answered, "Beauty is that which attracts your soul, and that which loves to give and not to receive. When you meet Beauty, you feel that the hands deep within your inner self are stretched forth to bring her into the domain of your heart. It is the magnificence[5] combined of sorrow and joy; it is the Unseen which you see, and the Vague which you understand, and the Mute which you hear—it is the Holy of Holies that begins in yourself and ends vastly beyond your earthly imagination."

Then the Nymph of the Jungle approached me and laid her scented hands upon my eyes. And as she withdrew, I found me alone in the valley. When I returned to the city, whose turbulence no longer vexed me, I repeated her words: "Beauty is that which attracts your soul, and that which loves to give and not to receive."

热词天地

1. clamor ['klæmə] *n.* 喧闹，叫嚷；大声的要求
2. entertaining [entə'teɪnɪŋ] *adj.* 令人愉快的
3. commemorate [kə'meməreɪt] *vt.* 庆祝，纪念；成为……的纪念
4. eternal [ɪ'tɜːnl] *adj.* 永恒的；不朽的
5. magnificence [mæg'nɪfɪsns] *n.* 壮丽；宏伟；富丽堂皇
   prevent ... from 防止……；预防……
   be committed to 致力于；委身于；以……为己任

在美神的宝座前

在繁忙的一天,我逃离了社会的冷脸、城镇的喧嚣,疲惫地走向那广阔的谷地。一时追逐小溪流水,一时聆听燕啭莺啼,直到一个僻静的地方,那里树木繁茂,遮天蔽日。

我在那儿站定,我的心灵被迷惑了——我那饥渴的心灵只看到生命的幻影而不是她的甜蜜。

我陷入沉思,在幻想的天地中自由翱翔。恍然时余,只见一位少女突然伫立在我面前。一根葡萄藤遮掩了她部分裸露的身体,金色的长发上戴着一顶罂粟花冠。她看出了我的愕然,招呼我说:"你别怕!我是丛林仙女。"

"像你这样的美女怎会委身于这个荒野?请告诉我你是谁,从哪里来?"我问道。她优雅地坐在绿草地上,答道:"我是大自然的象征。我就是你的祖先曾崇拜的那位神女,为了我的荣耀他们曾在巴勒贝克和朱拜勒为我建筑过祭坛和庙宇。"我鼓足勇气说:"但是那庙坛已是一片断壁残垣,我敬爱的祖先也已归于尘土,没有任何东西被留下来纪念他们的女神,在历史的断篇残简中也只能找到只言片语。"

她回答说:"有些女神因他们的崇拜者生而生,随着他们的死而死。然而有些却拥有永恒的生命。我的神性则来自于你随处可见的美丽世界。这种美就是大自然自身。这种美始自山坡之上牧人的愉快,田地中农人的幸福以及漂泊于山地间的部落的敬畏和满足。这种美促使智者登上真理的宝座。"

我又说道:"美是一种可怕的力量。"她即刻反驳道:"人类惧怕一切,甚至你们自己。你们惧怕天堂,那是你们精神安宁的家园;你们惧怕自然,那是平静和休憩的避风港;你们惧怕上帝的仁慈,指责他的愤怒,然而他却是充满了博爱与仁爱的主。"

一阵静默,夹杂着甜蜜的梦,然后我问道:"请给我讲讲究竟什么是美吧,人们对它的解说莫衷一是,各执己见;我也见到人们以各种方式来表达对它的尊敬与崇拜。"

她答道:"美是一种摄人心魄的东西,她甘愿给予,却不索取。当你遇见美,会感到内心深处向她伸出双手,想要揽她入怀,永存心间。她是悲喜交加的壮丽;她是见者无形,大音希声,心领神会的含糊——她是开启于你心灵深处的圣地,却终结于你世俗想象外的浩瀚之处……"

然后丛林仙女靠近我,将她芬芳的双手覆上我的眼帘。当她松开手时,我发现自己独自一人在山谷中。当我重返城市,它的喧嚣再也不能扰乱我心,我只是重复着她的话语:"美是一种摄人心魄的东西,她甘愿给予,却不索取。"

沙与沫 （冰心 译）

1

I am forever walking upon these shores,
Betwixt the sand and the foam.

The high tide will erase my foot-prints,
And the wind will blow away the foam.
But the sea and the shore will remain Forever.

我永远在沙岸上行走，
在沙土和泡沫的中间。

高潮会抹去我的脚印，风也会把泡沫吹走。
但是海洋和沙岸，却将永远存在。

2

We live only to discover beauty. All else is a form of waiting.

我们活着只为的是去发现美。
其他一切
都是等待的种种形式。

3

How shall my heart be unsealed[1] unless it be broken?

热词天地

1.unsealed [ˌʌnˈsiːld] *adj.* 未封口的；未证实的
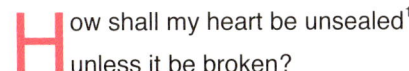 启封；解除约束（unseal 的过去分词）

我的心，除了把它敲碎以外，怎能把它打开呢？

4

Once I filled my hand with mist.
Then I opened it and lo, the mist was a worm.
And I closed and opened my hand again,
and behold there was a bird.
And again I closed and opened my hand,
and in its hollow stood a man
with a sad face, turned upward.
And again I closed my hand,
and when I opened it there was naught but mist.
But I heard a song of exceeding sweetness.

我曾抓起一把烟雾。
然后我伸掌一看，哎哟，
烟雾变成一个虫子。
我把手握起再伸开一看，
手里却是一只鸟。
我再把手握起又伸开，
在掌心里站着一个容颜忧郁、向天仰首的人。
我又把手握起，当我伸掌的时候，
除了烟雾以外，一无所有。
但是我听到了一支绝顶甜柔的歌曲。

5

It was but yesterday I thought myself fragment quivering
without rhythm in the sphere of life.

Now I know that I am the sphere,
and all life in rhythmic fragments moves within me.

仅仅在昨天,我认为我自己只是一个碎片,
无韵律地在生命的穹苍中颤抖。

现在我晓得,我就是那穹苍,
一切生命是在我里面有韵律地转动的碎片。

6

They say to me in their awakening,
"You and the world you live in are but a grain of sand upon the infinite shore of an infinite sea."

And in my dream I say to them,
"I am the infinite sea,
and all worlds are but grains of sand upon my shore."

他们在觉醒的时候对我说:
"你和你所居住的世界,
只不过是无边海洋的无边沙岸上的一粒沙子。"

在梦里我对他们说:
"我就是那无边的海洋,
大千世界只不过是我的沙岸上的沙粒。"

7

Only once have I been made mute.

It was when a man asked me, "Who are you?"

只有一次把我窘得哑口无言,

就是当一个人问我"你是谁"的时候。

8

The first thought of God was an angel.

The first word of God was a man.

想到神的第一个念头是一个天使。

说到神的第一个字眼是一个人。

9

We were fluttering, wandering,
longing creatures a thousand thousand years before the sea
and the wind in the forest gave us words.

Now how can we express the ancient of days
in us with only the sounds of our yesterdays?

我们是有海洋以前
千万年的扑腾着、飘游着、追求着的生物，
森林里的风把语言给予了我们。

那么我们怎能以昨天的声音
来表现我们心中的远古年代呢？

10

The Sphinx spoke only once,
and the Sphinx said,
"A grain of sand is a desert,
and a desert is a grain of sand;
and now let us all be silent again."

I heard the Sphinx,
but I did not understand.

斯芬克斯只说过一次话。
斯芬克斯说：
"一粒沙子就是一片沙漠，一片沙漠就是一粒沙子；
现在再让我们沉默下去吧。"

我听到了斯芬克斯的话，
但是我不懂得。

11

Long did I lie in the dust of Egypt,
silent and unaware of the seasons.

Then the sun gave me birth,
and I rose and walked upon the banks of the Nile,
Singing with the days and dreaming with the nights.

And now the sun threads upon me
with a thousand feet that I may lie again in the dust of Egypt.

But behold a marvel and a riddle!
The very sun that gathered me cannot scatter me.

Still erect am I,
and sure of foot do I walk upon the banks of the Nile.

我在埃及的沙土上躺了很久,
沉默着而且忘却了季节。

然后太阳把生命给了我,
我起来在尼罗河岸上行走。
和白天一同唱歌,和黑夜一同做梦。

现在太阳又用一千只脚在我身上践踏,
让我再在埃及的沙土上躺下。

但是,请看一个奇迹和一个谜吧!
那个把我集聚起来的太阳,
不能把我打散。

我依旧挺立着,
我以稳健的步履在尼罗河岸上行走。

12

We measure time according to the movement of countless suns;
and they measure time by little machines in their little pockets.

Now tell me,
how could we ever meet at the same place and the same time?

Space is not space between the earth and the sun
to one who looks down from the windows of the Milky Way.

我们依据无数太阳的运转来测定时间;
他们以他们口袋里的小小的机器来测定时间。

那么请告诉我,
我们怎能在同一的地点和同一的时间相会呢?

对于从银河的窗户里下望的人,
空间就不是地球与太阳之间的空间了。

13

Remembrance is a form of meeting.

Forgetfulness is a form of freedom.

记忆是相会的一种形式,

忘记是自由的一种形式。

14

Humanity is a river of light
running from the ex-eternity to eternity.

Do not the spirits who dwell in the ether
envy man his pain?

人性是一条光河,
从永久以前流向永久。

难道在以太里居住的精灵,
不妒羡世人的痛苦吗?

15

On my way to the Holy City
I met another pilgrim and I asked him,
"Is this indeed the way to the Holy City?"

And he said,
"Follow me, and you will reach the Holy City in a day and a night."
And I followed him.
And we walked many days and many nights,
yet we did not reach the Holy City.

And what was to my surprise
he became angry with me because he had misled me.

在到圣城去的路上,
我遇到另一位香客,我问他:
"这条就是到圣城去的路吗?"

他说:"跟我来吧,再有一天一夜就到达圣城了。"
我就跟随他,
我们走了几天几夜,
还没有走到圣城。

使我惊讶的是,
他带错了路反而对我大发脾气。

16

Make me, oh God,
the prey of the lion,
ere You make the rabbit my prey.

神呵,
让我做狮子的俘食,
要不就让兔子做我的俘食吧。

17

One may not reach the dawn save by the path of the night.

除了通过黑夜的道路,人们不能到达黎明。

18

My house says to me,
"Do not leave me, for here dwells your past."

And the road says to me,
"Come and follow me, for I am your future."

And I say to both my house and the road,
"I have no past, nor have I a future.
If I stay here, there is a going in my staying;
and if I go there is a staying in my going.
Only love and death will change all things."

How can I lose faith in the justice of life,
when the dreams of those who sleep upon feathers are not more beautiful
Than the dreams of those who sleep upon the earth?

我的房子对我说:
"不要离开我,因为你的过去住在这里。"

道路对我说:"跟我来吧,因为我是你的将来。"

我对我的房子和道路说:
"我没有过去,也没有将来。如果我住下来,我的住中就有去;如果我去,我的去中就有住。只有爱和死才能改变一切。"

当那些睡在绒毛上面的人所做的梦,
并不比睡在土地上的人的梦更美好的时候,
我怎能对生命的公平失掉信心呢?

19

In truth we talk only to ourselves, but sometimes we talk loud
enough that others may hear us.

实际上我们只对自己说话,
不过有时我们说得大声一点,
使得别人也能听见。

20

If the Milky Way were not within me how should I have seen it
or known it ?

假如银河不在我的意识里,我怎能看到它或了解它呢?

21

Unless I am a physician among physicians they would not believe
that I am an astronomer.

除非我是医生群中的一个医生,
他们不会相信我是一个天文学家的。

22

Perhaps the sea's definition of a shell is the pearl.
Perhaps time's definition of coal is the diamond.

也许大海给贝壳下的定义是珍珠。
也许时间给煤炭下的定义是钻石。

23

My friend, you and I shall remain strangers unto life,
And unto one another, and each unto himself,
Until the day when you shall speak and I shall listen,
Deeming your voice my own voice;
And when I shall stand before you,
Thinking myself standing before a mirror.

我的朋友,
你和我对于生命将永远是个陌生者,
我们彼此也是陌生者,
对自己也是陌生者,
直到你要说、我要听的那一天,
把你的声音作为我的声音;
当我站在你的面前,觉得我是站在镜前的时候。

24

Every great man I have known had something small in his make up;
and it was that small something which prevented inactivity or madness or suicide.

我所认得的大人物的性格中都有些渺小的东西;
就是这些渺小的东西,
阻止了懒惰、疯狂或者自杀。

25

The truly great man is he who would master no one,
and who would be mastered by none.

真正伟大的人是不压制人也不受人压制的人。

第二卷
生·死

先知 （冰心 译）

On Work

Then a ploughman said, "Speak to us of Work."
And he answered, saying:

You work that you may keep pace with the earth and the soul of the earth.

For to be idle is to become a stranger unto the seasons, and to step out of life's procession, that marches in majesty and proud submission[1] towards the infinite.

When you work you are a flute through whose heart the whispering of the hours turns to music.

Which of you would be a reed, dumb and silent, when all else sings together in unison?

Always you have been told that work is a curse and labor a misfortune.

But I say to you that when you work you fulfill a part of earth's furthest dream, assigned to you when that dream was born,

And in keeping yourself with labor you are in truth loving life,

And to love life through labor is to be intimate with life's inmost[2] secret.

But if you in your pain call birth an affliction and the support of the flesh a curse[3] written upon your brow, then I answer that naught but the sweat of your brow shall wash away that which is written.

You have been told also life is darkness, and in your weariness[4] you echo what was said by the weary.

And I say that life is indeed darkness save when there is urge,

And all urge is blind save when there is knowledge,

And all knowledge is vain save when there is work,

And all work is empty save when there is love;

And when you work with love you bind yourself to yourself, and to one another, and to God.

And what is it to work with love?

It is to weave the cloth with threads drawn from your heart, even as if your beloved were to wear that cloth.

It is to build a house with affection[5], even as if your beloved were to dwell in that house.

It is to sow seeds with tenderness and reap the harvest with joy, even as if your beloved were to eat the fruit.

It is to charge all things you fashion with a breath of your own spirit,

And to know that all the blessed dead are standing about you and watching.

Often have I heard you say, as if speaking in sleep, "He who works in marble, and finds the shape of his own soul in the stone, is nobler than he who ploughs the soil.

And he who seizes the rainbow to lay it on a cloth in the likeness of man, is more than he who makes the sandals for our feet."

But I say, not in sleep but in the over-wakefulness of noontide, that the wind speaks not more sweetly to the giant oaks than to the least of all the blades of grass;

And he alone is great who turns the voice of the wind into a song made sweeter by his own loving.

Work is love made visible.

And if you cannot work with love but only with distaste, it is better that you should leave your work and sit at the gate of the temple and take alms of those who work with joy.

For if you bake bread with indifference, you bake a bitter bread that feeds but half man's hunger.

And if you grudge[6] the crushing of the grapes, your grudge distils a poison in the wine.

And if you sing though as angels, and love not the singing, you muffle man's ears to the voices of the day and the voices of the night.

热词天地

1.submission [səb'mɪʃn] *n.* 投降；提交（物）；服从
2.inmost ['ɪnməʊst] *adj.* 心底的，内心深处的；最深的
3.curse [kɜːs] *n.* 诅咒；咒骂
4.weariness ['wɪərɪnəs] *n.* 疲倦，疲劳；
5.affection [ə'fekʃn] *n.* 喜爱，感情；影响；
6.grudge [grʌdʒ] *vt.* 怀恨；吝惜；妒忌；不情愿做　　*n.* 怨恨；恶意；妒忌

工作

于是一个农夫说:"请给我们谈工作。"
他回答说:

你工作为的是要与大地和大地的精神一同前进。
因为惰逸使你成为一个时代的生客、一个生命大队中的落伍者,这支大队是庄严的,高傲而服从的,向着无穷前进。

在你工作的时候,你是一管笛,从你心中吹出时光的微语,变成音乐。
你们谁肯做一根芦管,在万物合唱的时候,你独痴呆无声呢?

你们常听人说,工作是祸殃,劳动是不幸。
我却对你们说,你们工作的时候,你们完成了大地深远的梦之一部,他指示你那梦是从何时开头的。

而在你劳动不息的时候，你确实爱了生命。

在工作里爱了生命，就是通彻了生命最深的秘密。

倘然在你的辛苦里，将有身之苦恼和养身之诅咒，写上你的眉间，则我将回答你，只有你眉间的汗，能洗去这些字句。

你们也听见人说，生命是黑暗的。在你疲劳之中，你附和了那疲劳的人所说的话。

我说生命的确是黑暗的，除非是有了激励；

一切的激励都是盲目的，除非是有了知识；

一切的知识都是徒然的，除非是有了工作；

一切的工作都是空虚的，除非是有了爱。

当你仁爱地工作的时候，你便与自己、与人类、与上帝连系为一。

怎样才是仁爱的工作呢？

从你的心中抽丝织成布帛，仿佛你的爱者要来穿此衣裳。

热情地盖造房屋，仿佛你的爱者要住在其中。

温存地播种，欢乐地收刈，仿佛你的爱者要来吃这产物。

这就是用你自己灵魂的气息,来充满你所制造的一切。

要知道一切受福的古人,都在你上头看视着。

我常听见你们仿佛在梦中说:"那在蜡石上表现出他自己灵魂的形象的人,是比耕地的人高贵多了。

"那捉住虹霓,传神地画在布帛上的人,是比织履的人强多了。"

我却要说,不在梦中,而在正午清醒的时候,风对大橡树说话的声音,并不比对纤小的草叶所说的更甜柔;

只有那用他的爱心,把风声变成甜柔的歌曲的人,是伟大的。

工作是眼能看见的爱。

倘若你不是欢乐地却厌恶地工作,那还不如撇下工作,坐在大殿的门边,去乞求那些欢乐地工作的人的周济。

倘若你无精打采地烤着面包,你烤成的面包是苦的,只能救半个人的饥饿。

你若是怨重地压榨着葡萄酒,你的怨望,在酒里滴下了毒液。

倘若你能像天使一般地唱,却不爱唱,你就把人们能听到白天和黑夜的声音的耳朵都塞住了。

On Buying and Selling

And a merchant said, "Speak to us of Buying and Selling."
And he answered and said:

To you the earth yields her fruit, and you shall not want if you but know how to fill your hands.

It is in exchanging the gifts of the earth that you shall find abundance[1] and be satisfied.

Yet unless the exchange be in love and kindly justice[2], it will but lead some to greed and others to hunger.

When in the market place you toilers of the sea and fields and vineyards[3] meet the weavers and the potters and the gatherers of spices,—

Invoke[4] then the master spirit of the earth, to come into your midst and sanctify the scales and the reckoning that weighs value against value.

And suffer not the barren-handed to take part in your transactions, who would sell their words for your labor.

To such men you should say,

"Come with us to the field, or go with our brothers to the sea and cast your net;

For the land and the sea shall be bountiful to you even as to us."

And if there come the singers and the dancers and the flute players,—buy of their gifts also.

For they too are gatherers of fruit and frankincense, and that which they bring, though fashioned of dreams, is raiment and food for your soul.

And before you leave the marketplace, see that no one has gone his way with empty hands.

For the master spirit of the earth shall not sleep peacefully upon the wind till the needs of the least of you are satisfied.

热词天地

1.abundance [ə'bʌndəns] *n.* 充裕，丰富
2.justice ['dʒʌstɪs] *n.* 法官；司法；正义；公正
3.vineyard ['vɪnjəd] *n.* 葡萄园
4.Invoke [ɪn'vəʊk] *vt.* 调用；祈求；引起；恳求
　take part in 参加，参与

买卖

于是一个商人说:"请给我们谈买卖。"
他回答说:

大地贡献果实给你们,如果你们只晓得怎样独取,你们就不应当领受了。
在交易着大地的礼物里,你们将感到丰裕而满足。
然而若不是用爱和公平来交易,则必有人流为饕餮,有人流为饿殍。

当在市场上,你们这些海上、田中和葡萄园里的工人,遇见了织工、陶工和采集香料的——
就当祈求大地的主神,临到你们中间。来圣化天平,以及那较量价值的核算。
不要容许游手好闲的人来参加你们的买卖,他们会以言语来换取你们的劳力。
你们要对这种人说:
"同我们到田间,或者跟我们的兄弟到海上去撒网;
因为海与陆地,对你们也和对我们一样地慈惠。"

倘若那吹箫的和歌舞的人来了,你们也应当买他们的礼物。
因为他们也是果实和乳香的采集者,他们带来的物事,虽系梦幻,却是你们灵魂上的衣食。

在你们离开市场以前,要看着没有人空手回去。
因为大地主神,不到你们每人的需要全都满足了以后,他不能在风中宁静地睡眠。

On Teaching

Then said a teacher, "Speak to us of Teaching."
And he said:

No man can reveal to you aught but that which already lies half asleep in the dawning of your knowledge.

The teacher who walks in the shadow of the temple, among his followers, gives not of his wisdom but rather of his faith and his lovingness.

If he is indeed wise he does not bid[1] you enter the house of his wisdom, but rather leads you to the threshold[2] of your own mind.

The astronomer may speak to you of his understanding of space, but he cannot give you his understanding.

The musician may sing to you of the rhythm which is in all space, but he cannot give you the ear which arrests the rhythm nor the voice that echoes it.

And he who is versed in the science of numbers can tell of the regions of weight and measure, but he cannot conduct you thither[3].

For the vision of one man lends not its wings to another man.

And even as each one of you stands alone in God's knowledge, so must each one of you be alone in his knowledge of God and in his understanding of the earth.

热词天地

1.bid [bɪd] **vt.** 投标；出价；表示；吩咐　**vi.** 投标；吩咐　**n.** 出价；叫牌
2.threshold ['θreʃhəʊld] **n.** 入口；门槛；开始；极限；临界值
3.thither ['ðɪðə(r)] **adv.** 向那方；到那边
　be versed in 精通于

教授

于是一位教师说:"请给我们讲教授。"

他说:

除了那已经半睡着,躺卧在你知识的晓光里的东西之外,没有人能向你启示什么。

那在殿宇的阴影里,在弟子群中散步的教师,他不是在传授他的智慧,而是在传授他的忠信与仁慈。

假如他真是大智,他就不命令你进入他的智慧之堂,却要引导你到你自己心灵的门口。

天文家能给你讲述他对于太空的了解,他却不能把他的了解给你。

音乐家能给你唱出那充满太空的韵调,他却不能给你那聆受韵调的耳朵和应和韵调的声音。

精通数学的人能说出度量衡的方位,他却不能引导你到那方位上去。

因为一个人不能把他理想的翅翼借给别人。

正如上帝对于你们每个人的了解都是不相同的,所以你们对于上帝和大地的见解也应当是不相同的。

On Talking

And then a scholar said, "Speak of Talking."
And he answered, saying:

You can talk when you cease to be at peace with your thoughts;
And when you can no longer dwell in the solitude[1] of your heart you live in your lips, and sound is a diversion[2] and a pastime.

And in much of your talking, thinking is half murdered.
For thought is a bird of space, that in a cage of words may indeed unfold its wings but cannot fly.

There are those among you who seek the talkative[3] through fear of being alone.
The silence of aloneness reveals to their eyes their naked selves and they would escape.

And there are those who talk, and without knowledge or forethought reveal[4] a truth which they themselves do not understand.

And there are those who have the truth within them, but they tell it not in words.

In the bosom of such as these the spirit dwells in rhythmic silence.

When you meet your friend on the roadside or in the market place, let the spirit in you move your lips and direct your tongue.

Let the voice within your voice speak to the ear of his ear;

For his soul will keep the truth of your heart as the taste of the wine is remembered.

When the color is forgotten and the vessel is no more.

热词天地

1.solitude ['sɒlɪtjuːd] *n.* 孤独；隐居；荒僻的地方
2.diversion [daɪ'vɜːʃn] *n.* 转移；消遣；分散注意力
3.talkative ['tɔːkətɪv] *adj.* 饶舌的；多话的；多嘴的；爱说话的
4.reveal [rɪ'viːl] *vt.* 显示；透露；揭露；泄露
  in the bosom of 在（亲人）之间
  cease to be 不再是；停任

谈话

于是一个学者说:"请你讲讲谈话。"
他回答说:

在你不安于你的思想的时候,你就说话;
在你不能再在你心的孤寂中生活的时候,你就要在你的唇上生活,而声音是一种消遣,一种娱乐。

在你许多的谈话里,思想半受残害。
思想是天空中的鸟,在语言的笼里,也许会展翅,却不会飞翔。

你们中间有许多人,因为怕静,就去找多话的人。
在独居的寂静里,会在他们眼中呈现出他们赤裸的自己,他们就想逃避。
也有些说话的人,并没有知识和考虑,却要启示一种他们自己所不明白的真理。
也有些人的心里隐存着真理,他们却不用言语来诉说。
在这些人的胸怀中,心灵居住在有韵调的寂静里。
当你在道旁或市场遇见你朋友的时候,让你的心灵,运用你的嘴唇,指引你的舌头。
让你声音里的声音,对他耳朵的耳朵说话:
因为他的灵魂要嚼住你心中的真理。
如同酒光被忘却,酒杯也不存留,而酒味却永远被记念。

On Death

Then Almitra spoke, saying, "We would ask now of Death."
And he said:

You would know the secret of death.
But how shall you find it unless you seek it in the heart of life?
The owl whose night-bound eyes are blind unto[1] the day cannot unveil the mystery[2] of light.
If you would indeed behold the spirit of death, open your heart wide unto the body of life.
For life and death are one, even as the river and the sea are one.

In the depth of your hopes and desires lies your silent knowledge of the beyond[3];
And like seeds dreaming beneath the snow your heart dreams of spring.
Trust the dreams, for in them is hidden the gate to eternity.

Your fear of death is but the trembling[4] of the shepherd when he stands before the king whose hand is to be laid upon him in honor.
Is the shepherd not joyful beneath his trembling, that he shall wear the mark of the king?
Yet is he not more mindful of his trembling?

For what is it to die but to stand naked in the wind and to melt into the sun?

And what is it to cease breathing, but to free the breath from its restless tides, that it may rise and expand and seek God unencumbered[5]?

Only when you drink from the river of silence shall you indeed sing.

And when you have reached the mountain top, then you shall begin to climb.

And when the earth shall claim your limbs, then shall you truly dance.

热词天地

1. unto ['ʌntə] **prep.** 到,直到;向(等于 to)
2. mystery ['mɪstrɪ] **n.** 秘密,谜;神秘,神秘的事物
3. beyond [bɪ'jɒnd] **n.** 远处
4. trembling ['tremblɪŋ] **n.** 发抖
5. unencumbered [ˌʌnɪn'kʌmbəd] **adj.** 没有阻碍的;没有负担的
   melt into 溶解成;消散在……中;因心软而……

死

于是爱尔美差开口了,说:"现在我们愿意问'死'。"
他说:

你愿知道死的奥秘。
但是除了在生命的心中寻求以外,你们怎能寻见呢?
那夜中张目的枭鸟,它的眼睛在白昼是盲瞎的,不能揭露光明的神秘。
假如你真要瞻望死的灵魂,你当对生的肉体大大地开展你的心。
因为生和死是同一件事,如同江河与海洋也是同一件事。

在你的希望和愿欲的深处,隐藏着你对于来生的默识;
如同种子在雪下梦想,你们的心也在梦想着春天。
信赖一切的梦境吧,因为在那里面隐藏着永生之门。

你们的怕死,只是像一个牧人,当他站在国王的座前,被御手恩抚时的战栗。
在战栗之下,牧人岂不因为他身上已有了国王的手迹而喜悦么?
可是,他岂不更注意到他自己的战栗么?

除了在风中裸立,在日下消融之外,死还是什么呢?
除了把呼吸从不停的潮汐中解放,使它上升,扩大,无碍地寻求上帝之外,"气绝"又是什么呢?

只在你们从沉默的河中啜饮时,才真能歌唱。
只在你们达到山巅时,你们才开始攀援。
只在大地索取你们的四肢时,你们才真正地跳舞。

On Time

And an astronomer said, "Master, what of Time?"
And he answered:

You would measure time the measureless and the immeasurable.
You would adjust[1] your conduct and even direct the course of your spirit according to hours and seasons.
Of time you would make a stream upon whose bank you would sit and watch its flowing.

Yet the timeless[2] in you is aware of life's timelessness,
And knows that yesterday is but today's memory and tomorrow is today's dream.
And that which sings and contemplates[3] in you is still dwelling within the bounds of that first moment which scattered the stars into space.

Who among you does not feel that his power to love is boundless?
And yet who does not feel that very love, though boundless,

encompassed[4] within the centre of his being, and moving not from love thought to love thought, nor from love deeds to other love deeds?

And is not time even as love is, undivided and spaceless?
But if in your thought you must measure time into seasons, let each season encircle all the other seasons,
And let today embrace the past with remembrance and the future with longing.

热词天地

1. adjust [ə'dʒʌst] *vt.* 调整，使……适合；校准　*vi.* 调整，校准；适应
2. timeless ['taɪmləs] *adj.* 永恒的；不受时间影响的；不合时宜的
3. contemplate ['kɒntəmpleɪt] *vt.* 沉思；注视　*vi.* 冥思苦想；深思熟虑
4. encompass [ɪn'kʌmpəs] *vt.* 包含；包围，环绕；完成
   be aware of 意识到

时光

于是一个天文家说:"夫子,时光怎样讲呢?"他回答说:

你要测量那不可量、不能量的时间。

你要按照时辰与季候来调节你的举止,引导你的精神。

你要把时光当做一条溪水,你要坐在岸旁,看它流逝。

但那在你里面无时间性的"我",却觉悟到生命的无穷。

也知道昨日只是今日的回忆,而明日只是今日的梦想。

那在你里面歌唱着、默想着的,仍住在那第一刻在太空散布群星的圈子里。

你们中间谁不感到他的爱的能力是无穷的呢?

又有谁不感到那爱虽是无穷,却是在他本身的中心绕行,不是从这爱的思念移到那爱的思念,也不是从这爱的行为移到那爱的行为么?

而且时光岂不是也像爱,是不可分析,没有罅隙的么?

但若是在你的意想里,你定要把时光分成季候,那就让每一季候围绕住其他的季候。

也让今日用回忆拥抱着过去,用希望拥抱着将来。

泪与笑

The City of the Dead

Yesterday I drew myself from the noisome throngs and proceeded¹ into the field until I reached a knoll upon which Nature had spread her comely² garments. Now I could breathe.

I looked back, and the city appeared with its magnificent mosques and stately³ residences veiled by the smoke of the shops.

I commenced analyzing man's mission, but could conclude only that most of his life was identified with struggle and hardship. Then I tried not to ponder over what the sons of Adam had done, and centered my eyes on the field which is the throne of God's glory. In one secluded corner of the field I observed a burying ground surrounded by poplar trees.

There, between the city of the dead and the city of the living, I meditated. I thought of the eternal silence in the first and the endless sorrow in the second.

In the city of the living I found hope and despair; love and hatred, joy and sorrow, wealth and poverty, faith and infidelity.

In the city of the dead there is buried earth in earth that Nature converts, in the night's silence, into vegetation, and then into animal, and then into man.

As my mind wandered in this fashion, I saw a procession moving slowly and reverently, accompanied by pieces of music that filled the sky with sad melody. It was an elaborate funeral. The dead was followed by the living who wept and lamented his going. As the cortege reached the place of interment the priests commenced praying and burning incense, and musicians blowing and plucking their instruments, mourning the departed. Then the leaders came forward one after the other and recited their eulogies[4] with fine choice of words.

At last the multitude departed, leaving the dead resting in a most spacious and beautiful vault, expertly[5] designed in stone and iron, and surrounded by the most expensively-entwined wreaths of flowers.

The farewell-bidders returned to the city and I remained, watching them from a distance and speaking softly to myself while the sun was descending to the horizon and Nature was making her many preparations for slumber.

Then I saw two men laboring under the weight of a wooden casket, and behind them a shabby-appearing woman carrying an infant on her arms. Following last was a dog who, with heartbreaking eyes, stared first at the woman and then at the casket.

It was a poor funeral. This guest of Death left to cold society a miserable wife and an infant to share her sorrows and a faithful dog whose heart knew of his companion's departure.

As they reached the burial place they deposited the casket into a ditch away from the tended shrubs and marble stones, and retreated after a few simple words to God. The dog made one last turn to look at his friend's grave as the small group disappeared behind the trees.

I looked at the city of the living and said to myself, "That place belongs to the few." Then I looked upon the trim city of the dead and said, "That place, too, belongs to the few. Oh Lord, where is the haven of all the people?"

As I said this, I looked toward the clouds, mingled with the sun's longest and most beautiful golden rays. And I heard a voice within me saying, "Over there!"

热词天地

1. proceed [prə'si:d] *vi.* 开始；继续进行；发生；行进
2. comely ['kʌmlɪ] *adj.* 清秀的，标致的
3. stately ['steɪtlɪ] *adj.* 庄严的；堂皇的，宏伟的
4. eulogy ['ju:lədʒɪ] *n.* 悼词；颂词；颂扬；赞词
5. expertly ['ekspɜ:tlɪ] *adv.* 熟练地；巧妙地

逝者之城

昨天,我避开城市的喧嚣,信步原野,最终抵达一座小圆丘,大自然给那山丘披上了秀美的衣袍。现在,我终于可以自由呼吸。

我回望,整个城市连同它雄伟的清真寺和宏大的建筑都笼罩在店铺的烟云中。

我开始思忖人类的使命,结论却是他的生命大都伴随着奋斗和苦难。然后,我试图不再纠结于亚当子孙的所作所为,而是眺望原野,那是上帝荣耀的宝座。在原野的一个偏僻角落,我发现了一座杨树环绕着的陵园。

就在那里,在逝者之城与生者之城的中间,我陷入沉思。我想到了前者永恒之沉默与后者无尽之悲伤。

在生者之城,我发现了希望与绝望,热爱与憎恨,快乐与悲伤,财富与贫穷,信念与不忠。

在逝者之城,我只发现自然转化成的一抔黄土埋于黄土,在寂静的深夜,变成植物,然后是动物,再然后,成为人类。

就在我沉浸于种种遐想时,一队人群缓慢而恭敬地从我面前走过,伴着响亮的哀乐。那是一场冗长的葬礼。逝者身后是哭天抢地、为逝去哀悼的生者。当送葬队伍抵达陵园,神父们聚集起来,开始祈祷和焚香,乐师们也开始吹奏他们的乐器,哀悼逝者的离去。然后,引领者们依次上前诵读言辞华丽的悼词。

最后终于曲终人散,只剩逝者安息在最宽阔华美的墓穴里。那坟墓由石块和铁艺精心设计,被昂贵的缠枝花圈所围绕。

送殡的队伍返回城中,我仍在远处凝望他们,轻柔自语。太阳西沉,大自然已为安眠做好准备。

这时，我看见两个男人辛苦地抬着一口木棺，后面跟着一个衣衫破烂的妇人，怀里抱着一个婴儿。一只狗跟在最后面，带着心碎的眼神，先望向那妇人，又看向那口棺材。

这是一场穷人的葬礼。这个死亡之客留在冷酷世间的是一个悲惨的妻子，一个分担母亲悲伤的婴儿，还有一只内心深处知道主人已经离世的忠诚的狗。

这群人到了墓地，他们将棺材埋入一个沟槽，远离那精心修剪的灌木和大理石。一番简单地祷告后，他们就离去了。那只忠诚的狗向好朋友的长眠之地投去最后的回望，随队伍消失在树林后方。

这时，我望着生者之城，自言自语："那是属于少数富豪权贵的。"然后，我又看向逝者之地，自言自语："这个地方，也是属于少数富豪权贵的。那么，主啊！哪里是所有人的立身之地呢？"

我边想边眺望着漫天的晚霞，它被阳光镀了一道瑰丽的金边，只听见我心中有个声音说道："就在那里。"

A Poet's Death Is His Life

The dark wings of night enfolded the city upon which Nature had spread a pure white garment of snow; and men deserted[1] the streets for their houses in search of warmth, while the north wind probed in contemplation of laying waste the gardens. There in the suburb stood an old hut heavily laden with snow and on the verge of falling. In a dark recess of that hovel was a poor bed in which a dying youth was lying, staring at the dim light of his oil lamp, made to flicker by the entering winds. He a man in the spring of life who foresaw fully that the peaceful hour of freeing himself from the clutches of life was fast nearing. He was awaiting Death's visit gratefully, and upon his pale face appeared the dawn of hope; and on his lips a sorrowful smile; and in his eyes forgiveness.

He was poet perishing[2] from hunger in the city of living rich. He was placed in the earthly world to enliven the heart of man with his beautiful and profound sayings. He as noble soul, sent by the Goddess of Understanding to soothe[3] and make gentle the human spirit. But alas! He gladly bade the cold earth farewell without receiving a smile from its strange occupants.

He was breathing his last and had no one at his bedside save the oil lamp, his only companion, and some parchments upon which he had inscribed his heart's feeling. As he salvaged the remnants of his withering[4] strength he lifted his hands heavenward; he moved his eyes hopelessly, as if wanting to penetrate[5] the ceiling in order to see the stars from behind the veil clouds.

And he said, "Come, oh beautiful Death; my soul is longing for you.

Come close to me and unfasten the irons life, for I am weary of dragging them. Come, oh sweet Death, and deliver me from my neighbors who looked upon me as a stranger because I interpret to them the language of the angels. Hurry, oh peaceful Death, and carry me from these multitudes who left me in the dark corner of oblivion because I do not bleed the weak as they do. Come, oh gentle Death, and enfold me under your white wings, for my fellowmen are not in want of me. Embrace me, oh Death, full of love and mercy; let your lips touch my lips which never tasted a mother's kiss, not touched a sister's cheeks, not caresses a sweetheart's fingertips. Come and take me, by beloved Death."

Then, at the bedside of the dying poet appeared an angel who possessed a supernatural and divine beauty, holding in her hand a wreath of lilies. She embraced him and closed his eyes so he could see no more, except with the eye of his spirit. She impressed a deep and long and gently withdrawn kiss that left and eternal smile of fulfillment upon his lips. Then the hovel became empty and nothing was lest save parchments and papers which the poet had strewn with bitter futility.

Hundreds of years later, when the people of the city arose from the diseases slumber of ignorance and saw the dawn of knowledge, they erected a monument in the most beautiful garden of the city and celebrated a feast every year in honor of that poet, whose writings had freed them. Oh, how cruel is man's ignorance!

热词天地

1.desert ['dezət] *vt.* 遗弃；放弃；逃跑　*vi.* 遗弃；开小差；逃掉
2.perishing ['perɪʃɪŋ] *adj.* 讨厌的；糟糕的　*v.* 死亡（perish 的 ing 形式）；毁灭
3.soothe [su:ð] *vt.* 安慰；使平静；缓和　*vi.* 起抚慰作用
4.withering ['wɪðərɪŋ] *adj.* 使干枯的；使畏缩的；极有毁灭性的
5.penetrate ['penɪtreɪt] *vt.* 渗透；穿透；洞察　*vi.* 渗透；刺入；看透

诗人的死就是生

黑夜的翅翼笼罩着这座城市,它被自然披上了雪做的纯洁外衣。人们远离街头,躲在屋中寻求温暖。北风呼啸而过,思忖着如何荒废了花园。市郊有一座破旧的小屋,在冰雪之下摇摇欲坠。小屋一隅是一张破烂的床,上面躺着一个垂死的青年,正盯着油灯那暗淡的光。油灯在吹进屋内的寒风中闪烁。那是一位年华正盛的青年,他完全预见到了那使他摆脱生命之爪的宁静时刻即将来临。他耐心地等待着死神的降临,苍白的脸颊上浮现出了希望的曙光,唇边露出悲伤的微笑,眼中满是宽恕。

他是一位诗人,被派到世间,用那华美又深刻的语言使众人心旷神怡,如今却在满是富人的城中饿死。他是一个高尚的灵魂,上天派他降临人间,抚慰和软化人心。但如今啊,就要与尘世告别,他却未等到人们对他微笑。

在弥留之际,他尚存一息,床边无人陪伴,惟有孤灯是他唯一的伴侣。还有一页页的稿纸,纸上写的是他对心灵的感悟。那垂死的青年,聚集起最后的余力,向上苍举起两手,绝望地转动眼珠,仿佛是试图穿透那破败的屋顶,仰望苍穹中阴云遮盖的繁星。

然后，他说道："来吧，美丽的死神！我的灵魂早就对你神往。请靠拢过来，解开这生命的锁链，我拖着它早已筋疲力尽。来呀，亲爱的死神！解救我吧，带我离开这人间！这些邻居视我为异类，只因我向他们解读了天使之言。快来吧！宁静的死神！人类已经抛弃了我，将我掷于遗忘之渊，只因我不像他们那般贪婪，也不把弱者驱役。来呀，温柔的死神，用你白色的羽翼抱紧我，因为我的同胞不需要我。拥抱我吧，充满仁爱的死神，用你的唇亲吻我那未曾被母亲吻过的嘴唇，从未碰触过姐妹面颊的嘴唇，从未吻过心爱姑娘指尖的嘴唇。快来带走我吧，亲爱的死神！"

这时，他的床边，出现了一位天使，她拥有超脱自然的神圣之美，手握着百合花环。她走到他身边，俯身拥抱他，合上了诗人的双眼，使他只能用心灵之眼注视她。她在他的嘴唇上印了深深漫长的一吻，那爱怜之吻在他的唇上留下了永恒而满足的微笑。然后，小屋就空空如也，只剩尘土和羊皮纸，它们曾被诗人带着悲苦无奈地散落。

几百年后，当那座城市的居民从病态无知的睡眠中苏醒，看到知识的曙光，他们在城市最美的花园，为那位诗人树立了一座纪念碑，并每年集会表达对他的怀念，因为这位诗人的作品使他们得到了自由。啊，人的无知是多么的残酷啊！

沙与沫 （冰心 译）

1

Every seed is a longing.

每一粒种子都是一个愿望。

2

Death is not nearer to the aged than to the new-born; neither is life.

热词天地
the aged 老年人

死亡和老人的距离并不比和婴儿的距离更近；生命也是如此。

3

Mayhap[1] a funeral among men is a wedding feast among the angels.

热词天地

1.mayhap ['meɪhæp] *v.* 希望；但愿　*adv.* 也许

人间的葬礼也可能是天上的婚筵。

4

If the great-grandfather of Jesus had known what was hidden within him,
would he not have stood in awe of himself ?

如果耶稣的曾祖知道在他里面隐藏着的东西的话，他不会对自己肃然起敬吗？

5

Those who give you a serpent when you ask for a fish, may have nothing but serpents to give. It is then generosity[1] on their part.

热词天地

1.generosity [dʒenəˈrɒsətɪ] *n.* 慷慨，大方；宽宏大量

你向他们求鱼而却给你毒蛇的那些人，也许他们只有毒蛇可给。那么在他们一方面就算是慷慨的了。

6

I am ignorant of absolute truth.
But I am humble before my ignorance
and therein lies my honor and my reward.

There is a space between man's imagination
and man's attainment that may only be traversed by his longing.

Paradise is there, behind that door, in the next room;
but I have lost the key.
Perhaps I have only mislaid it.
You are blind and I am deaf and dumb,
so let us touch hands and understand.

我不知道什么是绝对的真理。
但是我对于我的无知是谦虚的,
这其中就有了我的荣誉和报酬。

在人的幻想和成就中间有一段空间,
只能靠他的热望来通过。

天堂就在那边,在那扇门后,在隔壁的房里;
但是我把钥匙丢了。
也许我只是把它放错了地方。
你瞎了眼睛,我是又聋又哑,
因此让我们握起手来互相了解吧。

7

Some of us are like ink and some like paper.

And if it were not for the blackness of some of us,
some of us would be dumb;
And if it were not for the whiteness of some of us,
some of us would be blind.

我们中间,有些人像墨水,有些人像纸张。

若不是因为有些人是黑的话,有些人就成了哑巴。
若不是因为有些人是白的话,有些人就成了瞎子。

8

Give me an ear and I will give you a voice.

给我一只耳朵,我将给你以声音。

9

Our mind is a sponge; our heart is a stream.

Is it not strange that most of us choose sucking rather than running?

我们的心才是一块海绵;我们的心怀是一道河水。

然而我们大多宁愿吸收而不肯奔流,这不是很奇怪吗?

10

When you long for blessings that you may not name,
and when you grieve knowing not the cause,
then indeed you are growing with all things that grow,
and rising toward your greater self.

当你想望着无名的恩赐，怀抱着无端的烦恼的时候，
你就真和一切生物一同长大，
升向你的大我。

11

When one is drunk with a vision, he deems his faint expression of it the very wine.

When my cup is empty I resign myself to its emptiness; but when it is half full I resent its half-fulness.

当一个人沉醉在一个幻象之中，他就会把这幻象的模糊的情味当做真实的酒。

当我的酒杯空了的时候，我就让它空着；但当它半满的时候，我却恨它半满。

12

The reality of the other person is not in what he reveals to you,
but in what he cannot reveal to you.

Therefore, if you would understand him,
listen not to what he says but rather to what he does not say.

Half of what I say is meaningless;
but I say it so that the other half may reach you.

一个人的实质,不在于他向你显露的那一面,
而在于他所不能向你显露的那一面。

因此,如果你想了解他,
不要去听他说出的话,而要去听他没有说出的话。

我说的话有一半是没有意义的;
我把它说出来,为的是也许会让你听到其他的一半。

13

A sense of humour is a sense of proportion.

幽默感就是分寸感。

14

My loneliness was born when men praised my talkative faults and blamed my silent virtues.

当人们夸奖我多言的过失,责备我沉默的美德的时候,我的寂寞就产生了。

15

When Life does not find a singer to sing her heart she produces a philosopher to speak her mind.

当生命找不到一个歌唱家来唱出她的心情的时候,她就产生一个哲学家来说出她的心思。

16

The voice of life in me cannot reach the ear of life in you; but let us talk that we may not feel lonely.

我的生命内的声音达不到你的生命内的耳朵；但是为了避免寂寞，就让我们交谈吧。

17

When two women talk they say nothing; when one woman speaks she reveals all of life.

当两个女人交谈的时候,她们什么话也没有说;
当一个女人自语的时候,她揭露了生命的一切。

18

If winter should say, "Spring is in my heart," who would believe winter?

如果冬天说,"春天在我的心里",谁会相信冬天呢?

19

Should you really open your eyes and see, you would behold your image in all images.

And should you open your ears and listen, you would hear your own voice in all voices.

如果你真的睁起眼睛来看,你会从每一个形象中看到你自己的形象。

如果你张开耳朵来听,你会在一切声音里听到你自己的声音。

20

It takes two of us to discover truth: one to utter it and one to understand it.

真理是需要我们两个人来发现的:一个人来讲说它,一个人来了解它。

21

Though the wave of words is forever upon us, yet our depth is forever silent.

虽然言语的波浪永远在我们上面喧哗,而我们的深处却永远是沉默的。

22

Many a doctrine is like a window pane. We see truth through it but it divides us from truth.

许多理论都像一扇窗户,我们通过它看到真理,但是它也把我们同真理隔开。

23

Now let us play hide and seek.
Should you hide in my heart it would not be difficult to find you.
But should you hide behind your own shell, then it would be useless for anyone to seek you.

让我们玩捉迷藏吧。
你如果藏在我的心里,就不难把你找到。
但是如果你藏到你的壳里去,那么任何人也找不到你。

24

A woman may veil her face with a smile.

一个女人可以用微笑把她的脸蒙了起来。

25

How noble is the sad heart who would sing a joyous song with joyous hearts.

那颗能够和欢乐的心一同唱出欢歌的忧愁的心,是多么高贵呵。

26

He who would understand a woman, or dissect genius, or solve the mystery of silence is the very man who would wake from a beautiful dream to sit at a breakfast table.

想了解女人,或分析天才,或想解答沉默的神秘的人,就是那个想从一个美梦中挣扎醒来坐到早餐桌上的人。

27

I would walk with all those who walk. I would not stand still to watch the procession passing by.

我愿意同走路的人一同行走。我不愿站住看着队伍走过。

28

You owe more than gold to him who serves you.
Give him of your heart or serve him.

对于服侍你的人，
你欠他的还不只是金子。
把你的心交给他或是服侍他吧。

29

If I were to choose between the power of writing a poem
and the ecstasy of a poem unwritten,
I would choose the ecstasy.

It is better poetry.

But you and all my neighbors agree that I always choose badly.

如果我在"写诗的能力"和"未写成诗的欢乐"之间选择的话,
我就要选那欢乐。

因为欢乐是更好的诗。

但是你和我所有的邻居,都一致地说我总是不会选择。

30

Should you care to write (and only the saints know why you should)
you must needs have knowledge and art and music
— the knowledge of the music of words, the art of being artless,
and the magic of loving your readers.

如果你要写作(只有圣人才晓得你为什么要写作),
你必须有知识、艺术和音乐
——字句的音乐的知识,
不矫揉造作的艺术,
和热爱你读者的魔术。

31

Nay, we have not lived in vain.
Have they not built towers of our bones?

没有,我们没有白活。
他们不是把我们的骨头堆成堡垒了吗?

32

Let us not be particular and sectional.
The poet's mind and the scorpion's tail rise in glory from the same earth.

我们不要挑剔计较吧。
诗人的心思和蝎子的尾巴,
都是从同一块土地上光荣地升起的。

33

Poetry is not an opinion expressed.
It is a song that rises from a bleeding wound or a smiling mouth.

诗不是一种表白出来的意见。
它是从一个伤口或是一个笑口涌出的一首歌曲。

34

Words are timeless.
You should utter them or write them with a knowledge of their timelessness.

言语是没有时间性的。
在你说它或是写它的时候应该懂得它的特点。

35

A poet is a dethroned king
sitting among the ashes of his palace
trying to fashion an image out of the ashes.

诗人是一个退位的君王,
坐在他的宫殿的灰烬里,
想用残灰捏出一个形象。

36

They dip their pens in our hearts and think they are inspired.

他们把笔蘸在我们的心怀里,就认为他们已经得了灵感了。

37

A scientist without imagination is a butcher with dull knives and out-worn scales.

But what would you,
since we are not all vegetarians ?

一个没有想象力的科学家,
好像一个拿着钝刀和旧秤的屠夫。

但既然我们不全是素食者,
那么你该怎么办呢?

38

The highest virtue here may be the least in another world.

这个世界里的最高德行,在另一个世界也许是最低的。

39

If it were not for our conception of weights and measures we would stand in awe of the firefly as we do before the sun.

如果不是因为我们有了重量和长度的观念,我们站在萤火光前也会同在太阳面前一样地敬畏。

40

When you sing the hungry hears you with his stomach.

当你歌唱的时候,饥饿的人就用他的肚子来听。

41

If indeed you must be candid, be candid beautifully;
Otherwise keep silent,
or there is a man in our neighborhood who is dying.

假如你必须直率地说的话,
就直率得漂亮一些。
要不就沉默下来,
因为我们邻近有一个人快死了。

42

Said a philosopher to a street sweeper,
"I pity you. Yours is a hard and dirty task."
And the street sweeper said,
"Thank you, sir. But tell me what is your task?"

And the philosopher answered saying,
"I study man's mind, his deeds and his desires."
Then the street sweeper went on with his sweeping
and said with a smile, "I pity you too."

一个哲学家对一个清道夫说：
"我可怜你，你的工作又苦又脏。"
清道夫说：
"谢谢你，先生。请告诉我，你做什么工作？"

哲学家回答说：
"我研究人的心思、行为和愿望。"
清道夫一面扫街一面微笑说：
"我也可怜你。"

43

They say to me,
"A bird in the hand is worth ten in the bush."
But I say,
"A bird and a feather in the bush is
worth more than ten birds in the hand."

Your seeking after that feather is life with winged feet;
nay, it is life itself.

他们对我说:"十鸟在树不如一鸟在手。"
我却说:"一鸟一羽在树胜过十鸟在手。"

你对那根羽毛的追求,就是脚下生翼的生命;
不,它就是生命的本身。

44

The flowers of spring are winter's dreams
related at the breakfast table of the angels.
Said a skunk to a tube-rose,
"See how swiftly I run, while you cannot walk nor even creep."

Said the tube-rose to the skunk,
"Oh, most noble swift runner,
please run swiftly!"

春天的花朵是天使们在早餐桌上所谈论的冬天的梦想。
鼬鼠对月下香说:
"看我跑得多快,你却不能走,也不会爬。"

月下香对鼬鼠说:
"啊,最高贵的快腿,请你快快跑开吧!"

第三卷
魂·物

先知 （冰心 译）

On Religion

And an old priest said, "Speak to us of Religion."
And he said:

Have I spoken this day of aught else?
Is not religion all deeds and all reflection[1],
And that which is neither deed nor reflection, but a wonder and a surprise ever springing in the soul, even while the hands hew the stone or tend the loom?

Who can separate his faith from his actions, or his belief from his occupation[2]?
Who can spread his hours before him, saying, "This for God and this for myself; This for my soul, and this other for my body?"
All your hours are wings that beat through space from self to self.

He who wears his morality but as his best garment were better naked.

The wind and the sun will tear no holes in his skin.

And he who defines his conduct by ethics[3] imprisons his song-bird in a cage.

The freest song comes not through bars and wires.

And he to whom worshipping is a window, to open but also to shut, has not yet visited the house of his soul whose windows are open from dawn to dawn.

Your daily life is your temple and your religion.

Whenever you enter into it take with you your all.

Take the plough and the forge and the mallet and the lute,

The things you have fashioned in necessity or for delight.

For in revery[4] you cannot rise above your achievements nor fall lower than your failures.

And take with you all men:

For in adoration you cannot fly higher than their hopes nor humble yourself lower than their despair.

And if you would know God be not therefore a solver of riddles.

Rather look about you and you shall see Him playing with your children.

And look into space; you shall see Him walking in the cloud, outstretching His arms in the lightning and descending in rain.

You shall see Him smiling in flowers, the rising and waving His hands in trees.

热词天地

1. reflection [rɪˈflekʃn] *n.* 反射；沉思；映象
2. occupation [ˌɒkjʊˈpeɪʃn] *n.* 职业；占有；消遣；占有期
3. ethics [ˈeθɪks] *n.* 伦理学；伦理观；道德标准
4. revery [ˈrevərɪ] *n.* 空想

   separate from 分离；把……和……分开

宗教

于是一个老道人说:"请给我们谈宗教。"
他说:

这一天中我曾谈过别的么?
宗教岂不是一切的功德、一切的反省,
或者那不是功德,也不是反省,只是在凿石或织布时灵魂中永远涌溢的一种叹异,一阵惊讶么?

谁能把他的信心和行为分开,把他的信仰和事业分开呢?
谁能把时间展现在面前,说"这时间是为上帝的,那时间是为我自己的;这时间是为我灵魂的,那时间是为我肉体的"呢?
你的一切光阴都是那在太空中鼓动的翅翼,从自我飞到自我。
那穿上"道德",只如同穿上他的最美的衣服的人,还不如赤裸着,
太阳和风不会把他的皮肤裂成洞孔。

把他的举止范定在伦理之内,是把善鸣之鸟囚在笼里。

最自由的歌声,不是从竹木弦线上发出的。

那以礼拜为窗户的人,开启而又关上,他还没有探访到他心灵之宫,那里的窗户是天天开启的。

你的日常生活,就是你的殿宇,你的宗教。

何时你进去,把你的一切都带了去。

带着犁耙和铁炉,木槌和琵琶,这些你为着需要或怡情而制造的物件。

因为在梦幻中,你不能超升到比你的成就还高,也不至于坠落到比你的失败还低。

你也要把一切的人都带着:

因为在钦慕上,你不能飞跃得比他们的希望还高,也不能卑屈得比他们的失望还低。

假如你要认识上帝,就不要做一个解谜的人。

不如举目四望,你将看见他同你的孩子们游戏。

也观看太空;你将看见他在云中行走,在电中伸臂,在雨中降临。

你将看见他在花中微笑,在树中举手挥动着。

On Self-Knowledge

And a man said, "Speak to us of Self-Knowledge."
And he answered, saying:

Your hearts know in silence the secrets of the days and the nights.
But your ears thirst for the sound of your heart's knowledge.
You would know in words that which you have always known in thought.
You would touch with your fingers the naked body of your dreams.
And it is well you should.

The hidden well-spring of your soul must needs rise and run murmuring to the sea;
And the treasure of your infinite depths would be revealed to your eyes.
But let there be no scales to weigh your unknown treasure;
And seek not the depths of your knowledge with staff or sounding line.
For self is a sea boundless and measureless.

Say not, "I have found the truth, " but rather, "I have found a truth."
Say not, "I have found the path of the soul." Say rather, "I have met the soul walking upon my path."
For the soul walks upon all paths.
The soul walks not upon a line, neither does it grow like a reed.
The soul unfolds itself, like a lotus of countless petals.

自知

于是一个男人说:"请给我们讲自知。"
他回答说:

在宁静中,你的心知道了白日和黑夜的奥秘。
但你的耳朵渴求听取你心的知识的声音。
你愿在意念中所了解的,能从语言中知道。
你愿能用手指去抚触你赤裸的梦魂。
你要这样做是好的。

你的心灵隐秘的涌泉,必须升溢,吟唱着奔向大海;
你的无穷深处的宝藏,必须在你目前呈现。
但不要用秤来衡量你的未知的珍宝,
也不要用杖竿和响带去探测你的知识的浅深。
因为自我乃是一个无边无际的海。

不要说"我找到了真理",只要说"我找到了一条真理"。
不要说"我找到了灵魂的道路",只要说"我遇见了灵魂在我的道路上行走。"
因为灵魂在一切的道路上行走。
灵魂不只在一条道上行走,也不是芦草似地生长。
灵魂如同一朵千瓣的莲花,自己开放着。

On Prayer

Then a priestess[1] said, "Speak to us of Prayer."
And he answered, saying:

You pray in your distress[2] and in your need; would that you might pray also in the fullness of your joy and in your days of abundance.

For what is prayer but the expansion of yourself into the living ether[3]?

And if it is for your comfort to pour your darkness into space, it is also for your delight to pour forth the dawning of your heart.

And if you cannot but weep when your soul summons you to prayer, she should spur[4] you again and yet again, though weeping, until you shall come laughing.

When you pray you rise to meet in the air those who are praying at that very hour, and whom save in prayer you may not meet.

Therefore let your visit to that temple invisible be for naught but ecstasy and sweet communion[5].

For if you should enter the temple for no other purpose than asking you shall not receive.

And if you should enter into it to humble yourself you shall not be lifted:

Or even if you should enter into it to beg for the good of others you shall not be heard.

It is enough that you enter the temple invisible.

I cannot teach you how to pray in words.

God listens not to your words save when He Himself utters[6] them through your lips.

And I cannot teach you the prayer of the seas and the forests and the mountains.

But you who are born of the mountains and the forests and the seas can find their prayer in your heart.

And if you but listen in the stillness of the night you shall hear them saying in silence, "Our God, who art our winged self, it is thy will in us that willeth.

"It is thy desire in us that desireth.

"It is thy urge in us that would turn our nights, which are thine, into days which are thine also.

"We cannot ask thee for aught, for thou knowest our needs before they are born in us:

"Thou art our need; and in giving us more of thyself thou givest us all."

热词天地

1. priestess ['pri:stes] *n.* 女祭司；神职人员
2. distress [dɪ'stres] *n.* 危难，不幸；贫困；悲痛
3. ether ['i:θə(r)] *n.* 乙醚；苍天；天空醚；以太
4. spur [spɜː(r)] *vi.* 骑马疾驰；给予刺激　*vt.* 激励，鞭策；给……装踢马刺
5. communion [kə'mju:nɪən] *n.* 共享；恳谈；宗教团体；圣餐仪式
6. utter ['ʌtə(r)] *vt.* 发出，表达；发射

祈祷

于是一个女祭司说:"请给我们谈祈祷。"
他回答说:

你们总在悲痛或需要的时候祈祷,我愿你们也在完满的欢乐中、幸福的日子里祈祷。

因为祈祷不就是你们的自我在活的"以太"中开展么?

假如向太空倾吐出你们心中的黑夜是个安慰,那么倾吐出你们心中的晓光也是个喜乐。

假若在你的灵魂命令你祈祷的时候,你只会哭泣,她也要从你的哭泣中反复地鼓励你,直到你笑悦为止。

在你祈祷的时候,你超凡高举,在空中你遇到了那些和你在同一时辰祈祷的人,除了那些祈祷时辰之外,你不会遇到的他们。

那么，让你那冥冥的殿宇的朝拜，只算个欢乐和甜柔的聚会罢。

因为假如你进入殿宇，除了请求之外，没有别的目的，你将不能接受。

假如你进入殿宇，只为要卑屈自己，你也并不被提高。

甚至于你进入殿宇，只为他人求福，你也不被嘉纳。

只要你进到了那冥冥的殿宇，这就够了。

我不能教给你们怎样用语言祈祷。

除了他通过你的嘴唇所说的他自己的言语之外，上帝不会垂听你的言语。

而且我也不能传授给你那大海、丛林和群山的祈祷。

但是你们生长在群山、丛林和大海之中的人，能在你们心中默会它们的祈祷。

假如你在夜的肃默中倾听，你会听见它们在严静中说：

"我们自己的'高我'的上帝，你的意志就是我们的意志。

"你的愿望就是我们的愿望。

"你的神力将会赐给我们的黑夜转为白日。

"我们不能向你求什么，因为在我们起念之前，你已知道了我们的需要。

"你是我们的需要，在你把自己已赐予我们的时候，你把一切都赐予我们了。"

On Eating and Drinking

Then an old man, a keeper of an inn, said, "Speak to us of Eating and Drinking."

And he said:

Would that you could live on the fragrance[1] of the earth, and like an air plant be sustained by the light.

But since you must kill to eat, and rob the newly born of its mother's milk to quench your thirst, let it then be an act of worship.

And let your board stand an altar on which the pure and the innocent of forest and plain are sacrificed for that which is purer and still more innocent in man.

When you kill a beast say to him in your heart,

"By the same power that slays you, I too am slain; and I too shall be consumed[2].

For the law that delivered[3] you into my hand shall deliver me into a mightier hand.

Your blood and my blood is naught but the sap that feeds the tree of heaven."

And when you crush an apple with your teeth, say to it in your heart,

"Your seeds shall live in my body,

And the buds of your tomorrow shall blossom in my heart,

And your fragrance shall be my breath,
And together we shall rejoice through all the seasons."

And in the autumn, when you gather the grapes of your vineyards for the winepress, say in your heart,

"I too am a vineyard, and my fruit shall be gathered for the winepress,

And like new wine I shall be kept in eternal vessels."

And in winter, when you draw the wine, let there be in your heart a song for each cup;

And let there be in the song a remembrance for the autumn days, and for the vineyard, and for the winepress.

热词天地

1.fragrance ['freɪgrəns] *n.* 香味，芬芳
2.consume [kən'sju:m] *vt.* 消耗；使……著迷；挥霍 *vi.* 耗尽，毁灭；耗尽生命
3.deliver [dɪ'lɪvə(r)] *vt.* 交付；发表；递送 *vi.* 实现；传送；履行；投递
 sacrifice for 为……作出牺牲

饮食

一个开饭店的老人说:"请给我们谈饮食。"
他说:

我恨不得你们能依靠大地的香气而生存,如同那空气植物受着阳光的供养。

既然你们必须杀生为食,而且从新生的动物口中夺他的母乳来止渴,那就让它成为一个敬神的礼节罢。

让你的肴馔摆在祭坛上,那是丛林中和原野上的纯洁清白的物品,为更纯洁清白的人们而牺牲的。

当你杀生的时候,心里对他说:
"在宰杀你的权力之下,我同样地被宰杀,我也要同样地被吞食。
那把你送到我手里的法律,也要把我送到那更伟大者的手里。
你和我的血都不过是浇灌天树的一种液汁。"

当你咬嚼着苹果的时候,心里对它说:
"你的子核要在我身中生长,
你来世的嫩芽要在我心中萌茁,
你的芬香要成为我的气息,
我们要终年地喜乐。"

在秋天,你在果园里摘葡萄榨酒的时候,心里说:
"我也是一座葡萄园,我的果实也要摘下榨酒,
和新酒一般,我也要被收存在永生的杯里。"
在冬日,当你斟酒的时候,你的心要对每一杯酒歌唱;
让那歌曲成为一首纪念秋天和葡萄园以及榨酒之歌。

On Houses

Then a mason came forth and said, "Speak to us of Houses."
And he answered and said:

Build of your imaginings a bower in the wilderness ere[1] you build a house within the city walls.

For even as you have home-comings in your twilight[2], so has the wanderer in you, the ever distant and alone.

Your house is your larger body.

It grows in the sun and sleeps in the stillness of the night; and it is not dreamless.

Does not your house dream? And dreaming, leave the city for grove or hilltop?

Would that I could gather your houses into my hand, and like a sower scatter them in forest and meadow.

Would the valleys were your streets, and the green paths your

alleys, that you might seek one another through vineyards, and come with the fragrance of the earth in your garments.

But these things are not yet to be.

In their fear your forefathers gathered you too near together. And that fear shall endure[3] a little longer. A little longer shall your city walls separate your hearths from your fields.

And tell me, people of Orphalese, what have you in these houses? And what is it you guard with fastened doors?

Have you peace, the quiet urge that reveals your power?

Have you remembrances, the glimmering arches that span the summits of the mind?

Have you beauty, that leads the heart from things fashioned of wood and stone to the holy mountain?

Tell me, have you these in your houses?

Or have you only comfort, and the lust for comfort, that stealthy thing that enters the house a guest, and then becomes a host, and then a master?

Ay, and it becomes a tamer, and with hook and scourge makes puppets of your larger desires.

Though its hands are silken, its heart is of iron.

It lulls you to sleep only to stand by your bed and jeer at the dignity[4] of the flesh.

It makes mock of your sound senses, and lays them in thistledown like fragile vessels.

Verily the lust for comfort murders the passion of the soul, and then walks grinning in the funeral.

But you, children of space, you restless in rest, you shall not be trapped nor tamed.

Your house shall be not an anchor but a mast.

It shall not be a glistening film that covers a wound, but an eyelid that guards the eye.

You shall not fold your wings that you may pass through doors, nor bend your heads that they strike not against a ceiling, nor fear to breathe lest walls should crack and fall down.

You shall not dwell in tombs made by the dead for the living.

And though of magnificence and splendour, your house shall not hold your secret nor shelter your longing.

For that which is boundless in you abides in the mansion of the sky,whose door is the morning mistand whose windows are the songs and the silences of night.

热词天地

1.ere [eə(r)] *prep.* 在……以前；毋宁
2.twilight ['twaɪlaɪt] *n.* 黎明，黄昏；薄暮；衰退期；朦胧状态
3.endure [ɪn'djʊə(r)] *vi.* 忍耐；持续
4.dignity ['dɪɡnəti] *n.* 尊严；高贵
   separate...from 分离；把……和……分开
   jeer at 嘲笑；嘲弄；戏弄

居室

于是一个泥水匠走上前来说:"请给我们谈居室。"
他回答说:

当你在城里盖一所房子之前,先在野外用你的想象盖一座凉亭。

因为你黄昏时有家可归,而你那更迷茫、更孤寂的漂泊的精魂,也有个归宿。

你的房屋是你的较大的躯壳。

他在阳光中发育,在夜的寂静中睡眠;而且不能无梦。

你的房屋不做梦么?不梦见离开城市,登山入林么?

我愿能把你们的房子聚握在手里,撒种似的把他们洒落在丛林中与绿野上。

愿山谷成为你们的街市,绿径成为你们的里巷,使你们在葡萄园中相寻相访的时候,衣袂上带着大地的芬芳。

但这个还一时做不到。

在你们祖宗的忧惧里,他们把你们聚集得太近了。这忧惧还要稍微延长,你们的城墙,也仍要把你们的家庭和你们的田地分开的。

告诉我罢,阿法利斯的民众呵,你们的房子里有什么?你们锁门是为守护什么呢?

你们有"和平",不就是那呈露你魄力的宁静和鼓励么?

你们有"回忆",不就是那连跨你心峰的灿烂的弓桥么?

你们有"美",不就是那把你的心从木石建筑上引到圣山的么?

告诉我,你们的房屋里有这些东西么?

或者你只有"舒适"和"舒适的欲念",那诡秘的东西,以客人的身份混了进来渐作家人,终作主翁的么?

嘻,他变成一个驯兽的人,用钩镰和鞭笞,使你较伟大的愿望变成傀儡。

他的手虽柔软如丝,他的心却是铁打的。

他催眠你,只须站在你的床侧,讥笑你肉体的尊严。

他戏弄你健全的感官,把它们塞放在蓟绒里,如同脆薄的杯盘。

真的,舒适之欲,杀害了你灵性的热情,又哂笑地在你的殡仪队中徐步。

但是你们这些"太空"的儿女,你们在静中不息,你们不应当被网罗,被驯养。

你们的房子不应当做个锚,却应当做个桅。

它不应当做一片遮掩伤痕的闪亮的薄皮,却应当做那保护眼睛的睫毛。

你不应当为穿门走户而敛翅,也不应当为恐触到屋顶而低头,也不应当为怕墙壁崩裂而停止呼吸。

你不应当住在那死人替活人筑造的坟墓里。

无论你的房屋是如何地壮丽与辉煌,也不应当使它隐住你的秘密,遮住你的愿望。

因为你里面的"无穷性",是住在天宫里,那天宫是以晓烟为门户,以夜的静寂与歌曲为窗牖的。

On Clothes

And the weaver said, "Speak to us of Clothes."
And he answered:

Your clothes conceal[1] much of your beauty, yet they hide not the unbeautiful.

And though you seek in garments the freedom of privacy you may find in them a harness and a chain.

Would that you could meet the sun and the wind with more of your skin and less of your raiment,

For the breath of life is in the sunlight and the hand of life is in the wind.

Some of you say, "It is the north wind who has woven the clothes we wear."

And I say, Ay, it was the north wind,

But shame was his loom², and the softening of the sinews was his thread.

And when his work was done he laughed in the forest.

Forget not that modesty is for a shield³ against the eye of the unclean.

And when the unclean shall be no more, what were modesty but a fetter and a fouling of the mind?

And forget not that the earth delights to feel your bare feet and the winds long to play with your hair.

热词天地

1.conceal [kən'siːl] *vt.* 隐藏;隐瞒
2.loom [luːm] *n.* 织布机;若隐若现的景象
3.shield [ʃiːld] *n.* 盾;防护物;保护者

衣服

于是一个织工说:"请给我们谈衣服。"
他回答说:

你们的衣服掩盖了许多的美,却遮不住丑恶。
你们虽可在衣服里找到隐秘的自由,却也找到了橛饰与羁勒了。
我恨不得你们多用皮肤而少用衣服去迎接太阳和风。
因为生命的气息是在阳光中,生命的把握是在风里。
你们中有人说:"那纺织衣服给我们穿的是北风。"
我也说:对的,是北风,
但他的机杼是可羞的,那使筋肌软弱的是他的线缕。
当他的工作完毕时,他在林中喧笑。

不要忘却,"羞怯"只是遮挡"不洁"的眼目的盾牌。
在"不洁"完全没有了的时候,"羞怯"不是仅仅是心上的桎梏与束缚么?
也别忘了大地是欢喜和你的赤脚接触,风是希望和你的头发相戏的。

泪与笑

Vision

There in the middle of the field, by the side of a crystalline[1] stream, I saw a bird-cage whose rods and hinges were fashioned[2] by an expert's hands. In one corner lay a dead bird, and in another were two basins—one empty of water and the other of seeds.

I stood there reverently, as if the lifeless bird and the murmur of the water were worthy of deep silence and respect—something worth of examination and meditation by the heard and conscience[3].

As I engrossed myself in view and thought, I found that the poor creature had died of thirst beside a stream of water, and of hunger in the midst of a rich field, cradle of life; like a rich man locked inside his iron safe, perishing from hunger amid heaps of gold.

Before my eyes I saw the cage turned suddenly into a human skeleton, and the dead bird into a man's heart which was bleeding from a deep wound that looked like the lips of a sorrowing woman.

A voice came from that wound saying, "I am the human heart, prisoner of substance and victim of earthly laws.

"In God's field of Beauty, at the edge of the stream of life, I was imprisoned in the cage of laws made by man.

"In the center of beautiful Creation I died neglected because I was kept from enjoying the freedom of God's bounty.

"Everything of beauty that awakens my love and desire is a disgrace[4], according to man's conceptions; everything of goodness that I crave is but naught, according to his judgment.

"I am the lost human heart, imprisoned in the foul dungeon of man's dictates, tied with chains of earthly authority, dead and forgotten by laughing humanity whose tongue is tied and whose eyes are empty of visible tears."

All these words I heard, and I saw them emerging with a stream of ever thinning blood from that wounded heart.

More was said, but my misted eyes and crying should prevented further sight or hearing.

热词天地

1. crystalline ['krɪstəlaɪn] *adj.* 透明的；水晶般的；水晶制的
2. fashion ['fæʃn] *vt.* 制作，塑造；使适应
3. conscience ['kɒnʃəns] *n.* 道德心，良心
4. disgrace [dɪs'ɡreɪs] *n.* 耻辱；丢脸的人或事；失宠
   bleed from 血从……流出

梦

在田野中,一条澄澈的小溪旁,我看到一只鸟笼,那笼子由能工巧匠精心编织而成。笼子的一角躺着一只死去的小鸟,另一角有两只小盆——一只滴水未留,另外一只也稻米尽空。

我恭敬地伫立,恍如没有生命的小鸟,以及潺潺的水声也值得静默与尊重——值得用心灵和良知去冥思探询。

当我用心察看时,我发现,这可怜的小东西在溪水边,却死于干渴;它在生命的摇篮——丰裕的原野中央,却死于饥饿。犹如一个财主,被锁于铁制的金库,饿死在成堆的金子里。

就在我眼前,那笼子变成了一具骷髅,那死去的小鸟变成了一颗人心,那心上有一个深深的伤口,流着殷红的鲜血,如一个悲伤的女人的唇。

随后,从那伤口中传出这样的话语:"我是人类的心,是物质的俘虏,是尘世俗陋习的受害者。在上帝那美丽的田野里,在生命的溪流旁,我被关进人造的法规樊笼;在美丽的造物中心,我默默地死去。因为我被拒绝享有上帝赐予的自由。据世俗的观念,所有能唤醒我爱与渴望的美物,都是可耻的;根据人类的判断,所有我热切追求的美德,不过是一场徒劳。

"我是失落的人心,被囚禁在世俗陈规的恶臭地牢,被世俗权威的锁链捆绑,已然死去,并被嘲笑的人们所遗忘。他们的舌头打了结,不能说话,双目空洞,看不到一滴泪。"

我听了这些话语,看见它们是出自那颗受伤的心,连同鲜血滴滴。更多的话语还在继续,而我愈发模糊的眼和发出的呼喊,使我再也看不到,也听不到了。

Song of the Wave

The strong shore is my beloved
And I am his sweetheart.
We are at last united by love, and
Then the moon draws me from him.
I go to him in haste and depart
Reluctantly[1], with many
Little farewells.

I steal swiftly from behind the
Blue horizon to cast the silver of
My foam[2] upon the gold of his sand, and
We blend in melted brilliance.

I quench his thirst and submerge his
Heart; he softens my voice and subdues[3]
My temper.
At dawn I recite the rules of love upon

His ears, and he embraces me longingly.
At eventide I sing to him the song of
Hope, and then print smooth hisses upon
His face; I am swift and fearful, but he
Is quiet, patient, and thoughtful. His
Broad bosom soothes my restlessness.

As the tide comes we caress each other,
When it withdraws, I drop to his feet in
Prayer.

Many times have I danced around mermaids
As they rose from the depths and rested
Upon my crest to watch the stars;
Many times have I heard lovers complain
Of their smallness, and I helped them to sigh.

Many times have I teased the great rocks
And fondled them with a smile, but never
Have I received laughter from them;
Many times have I lifted drowning souls

And carried them tenderly to my beloved
Shore. He gives them strength as he
Takes mine.

Many times have I stolen gems from the
Depths and presented them to my beloved
Shore. He takes them in silence, but still
I give fro he welcomes me ever.

In the heaviness of night, when all
Creatures seek the ghost of Slumber, I
Sit up, singing at one time and sighing
At another. I am awake always.

Alas! Sleeplessness has weakened me!
But I am a lover, and the truth of love
Is strong.
I may be weary, but I shall never die.

热词天地

1.reluctantly [rɪ'lʌktəntlɪ] *adv.* 不情愿地；嫌恶地
2.foam [fəʊm] *n.* 泡沫；水沫；灭火泡沫
3.subdue [səb'dju:] *vt.* 征服；抑制；减轻

浪之歌

雄伟的海岸是我的爱人，我是他的心肝儿，我们甜蜜如一，皎月却使我们分离。聚散匆匆，尽是离情别意。

我从蓝色地平线的背后迅速潜出，为了将我泡沫中的银花，掷于他海岸的金沙上，我们在灿烂中融为一体。

我除去他的饥渴，潜入他的心扉，他柔化我的声音，制服我的怒气。拂晓时，我在他的耳边叮咛爱的规矩，他热情的拥抱不让我离去。黄昏时，我为他吟唱希望之歌，在他的脸颊印上我柔和的气息。我急切又彷徨，他却沉静、耐心又周详。他宽厚的胸膛，舒缓着我的躁动与慌张。

潮涨时，我们爱抚拥抱；潮落时，我在祷告中膜拜在他的脚踝。

曾有多少次，我在美人鱼的身畔翩跹起舞。她们浮现于海底，栖息在我的峰顶仰望繁星。曾有多少次，我听到恋人们慨叹着自身的渺小，陪他们一同嗟叹。

曾有多少次，我逗弄那巨岩，含笑抚摸，却从未收到笑语回眸。曾有多少次，我托起那溺水的灵魂，温柔地送回到我热恋的海岸。他给他们以力量，正如从我这里拿走的。

曾有多少次，我从深海窃得珍宝，献给我热恋的海岸，他默默收下，我仍继续给予，因为他对我一如既往地欢迎。

夜阑人静，当万物都去寻觅休眠之灵时，我坐起来，时唱时叹，总是一夜无眠。

唉！不眠已使我形容憔悴。但我满心是爱情，而爱情的真谛是坚定。也许我会疲倦，却永不会死亡。

The Creation

The God separated a spirit from Himself and fashioned it into Beauty. He showered upon her all the blessings of gracefulness and kindness. He gave her the cup of happiness and said, "Drink not from this cup unless you forget the past and the future, for happiness is naught but the moment." And He also gave her a cup of sorrow and said, "Drink from this cup and you will understand the meaning of the fleeting[1] instants of the joy of life, for sorrow ever abounds."

And the God bestowed[2] upon her a love that would desert he forever upon her first sigh of earthly satisfaction, and a sweetness that would vanish with her first awareness of flattery.

And He gave her wisdom from heaven to lead to the all-righteous[3] path, and placed in the depth of her heart and eye that sees the

unseen, and created in he an affection and goodness toward all things. He dressed her with raiment of hopes spun by the angels of heaven from the sinews of the rainbow. And He cloaked her in the shadow of confusion, which is the dawn of life and light.

Then the God took consuming fire from the furnace of anger, and searing wind from the desert of ignorance, and sharp-cutting sands from the shore of selfishness, and coarse earth from under the feet of ages, and combined them all and fashioned Man. He gave to Man a blind power that rages and drives him into a madness which extinguishes[4] only before gratification of desire, and placed life in him which is the specter of death.

And the God laughed and cried. He felt an overwhelming[5] love and pity for Man, and sheltered him beneath His guidance.

热词天地

1. fleeting ['fliːtɪŋ] *adj.* 飞逝的；转瞬间的
2. bestow [bɪ'stəʊ] *vt.* 使用；授予；放置；留宿
3. righteous ['raɪtʃəs] *adj.* 正义的；正直的；公正的
4. extinguish [ɪk'stɪŋɡwɪʃ] *vt.* 熄灭；压制；偿清
5. overwhelming [əʊvə'welmɪŋ] *adj.* 势不可挡的，压倒一切的，巨大的；

造物

造物主从自身分离出一个灵魂,并将之塑造为美人。他对她施以优雅和仁慈的祝福。他给予她一杯幸福之酒说道:"除非你遗忘过去,不顾未来,否则不要喝下这杯酒,因为幸福只在当下。"他又给她一杯悲伤之酒,说道:"喝下它,你就会珍惜生活中所有转瞬即逝的欢乐,因为悲伤比比皆是。"

主赐予她爱,一旦她发出世俗满足的轻叹,那爱就会永远消失;主赐给她以甜蜜,然而一旦她感受到阿谀之辞,甜蜜也会消失殆尽。

主赐予她来自天堂的智慧,深植于心灵和眼睛,使她体察于无形,带她走上真理之路;主给她注入对万物的喜爱和慈悲之情;给她穿上来自彩虹要塞的天使编织的希望彩衣。随后,主给她披上困惑的阴影,而那暗影正孕育着黎明之光。

主从愤怒之炉取出烈火,从无知的沙漠掳来强风,从自私的海滩掘出尖利沙石,从岁月的足底挖来粗糙泥土,并将它们糅合,塑造了男人。他给予男人盲目的权力:这权力使他暴怒和疯狂,这欲火直到满足才熄灭;然后,主又给他注入生命,这生命同时也是死亡的幽灵。

主悲喜交集,对男人他感到无限的爱与怜悯,并一路引导庇护着他。

Song of the Rain

I am dotted silver threads dropped from heaven
By the Gods. Nature then takes me, to adorn[1]
Her fields and valleys.
I am beautiful pearls, plucked from the
Crown of Ishtar by the daughter of Dawn
To embellish[2] the gardens.
When I cry the hills laugh;
When I humble myself the flowers rejoice;
When I bow, all things are elated.
The field and the cloud are lovers
And between them I am a messenger of mercy.
I quench the thirst of one;
I cure the ailment of the other.
The voice of thunder declares my arrival;
The rainbow announces my departure[3].
I am like earthly life, which begins at
The feet of the mad elements and ends
Under the upraised wings of death.
I emerge from the heard of the sea
Soar with the breeze. When I see a field in
Need, I descend and embrace the flowers and
The trees in a million little ways.
I touch gently at the windows with my
Soft fingers, and my announcement is a
Welcome song. All can hear, but only

The sensitive can understand.

The heat in the air gives birth to me,

But in turn I kill it,

As woman overcomes man with

The strength she takes from him.

I am the sigh of the sea;

The laughter of the field;

The tears of heaven.

So with love—

Sighs from the deep sea of affection;

Laughter from the colorful field of the spirit;

Tears from the endless heaven of memories.

热词天地

1.adorn [ə'dɔːn] *vt.* 装饰；使生色
2.embellish [ɪm'belɪʃ] *vt.* 修饰；装饰；润色
3.departure [dɪ'pɑːtʃə(r)] *n.* 离开；出发；违背
   drop from 从……落下；从……除去
   pluck from 从……拔出来
   emerge from 自……出现；从……显露出来

雨之歌

我是众神从天撒落的银色珠串,自然于是用我装扮她的田野与山谷。

我是美丽的珍珠,黎明的女儿从伊什塔的皇冠上将我采下,用来点缀花园。

当我哭泣时,群山欢笑;当我谦卑时,花朵欢欣;当我鞠躬时,万物欢畅。

原野和云朵是恋人,我是它们之间传情的信使。我为一个解渴,为另一个除去小恙。

雷声宣告我的降临;彩虹通报我的离去。我喜欢世俗的生活,诞生在疯狂的脚下,又在死亡飘起的羽翼下终结。

我从涛声中升起,乘轻风翱翔云天。每当看到田野的渴求,我便飘落而下,以万般姿态拥抱花朵和树林。

我用柔柔纤指,轻拂扇扇窗棂,我的宣言是一曲欢迎之歌。谁都能听到,却只有善感之心才能听懂。

空气的燥热孕育我,我却让它逝去无踪,正如一个女人,用从男人那儿获取的力量来征服他。

我是大海的叹息;是田野的欢笑;是天空的眼泪。

于是,满含爱意——来自爱情深海的叹息;
笑声自斑斓的精神原野放飞;
眼泪自无边的记忆天堂洒落。

Song of the Flower

I am a kind word uttered[1] and repeated
By the voice of Nature;
I am a star fallen from the
Blue tent upon the green carpet.
I am the daughter of the elements
With whom Winter conceived[2];
To whom Spring gave birth; I was
Reared[3] in the lap of Summer and I
Slept in the bed of Autumn.

At dawn I unite with the breeze
To announce the coming of light;
At eventide[4] I join the birds
In bidding the light farewell.

The plains are decorated with
My beautiful colors, and the air
Is scented with my fragrance.

As I embrace slumber the eyes of
Night watch over me, and as I
Awaken I stare at the sun, which is
The only eye of the day.

I drink dew[5] for wine, and hearken to
The voices of the birds, and dance
To the rhythmic swaying of the grass.
I am the lover's gift; I am the wedding wreath;
I am the memory of a moment of happiness;
I am the last gift of the living to the dead;
I am a part of joy and a part of sorrow.

But I look up high to see only the light,
And never look down to see my shadow.
This is wisdom which man must learn.

热词天地

1.utter ['ʌtə(r)] *vt.* 发出声音；说，讲
2.conceive [kən'si:v] *vt.* & *vi.* 怀孕；构思；想像，设想
3.rear [rɪə(r)] *vt.* 饲养；养育；抚养；养育
4.eventide ['i:vntaɪd] *n.* <古><诗> 黄昏，日暮
5.dew [dju:] *n.* 水珠，露水
  watch over 看守，监视

花之歌

我是自然亲切的反复呢喃；
我是一颗星，
从蓝色苍穹坠落在绿色地毯。
我是元素之女：
在冬天里孕育；
在春天里出生；
在夏天成长；
在秋天安睡。

黎明，我同清风一道，
宣告光明的到来；
傍晚，与群鸟一起，
为光明的远去告别。

我美丽的色彩，
装饰了原野；

我的芬芳,
使空气馥郁。

我沉睡时,
夜色将我关照;
我醒来时,
就注视太阳这白昼唯一的眼。

我饮朝露酿成的琼浆;
听着鸟儿的婉转歌唱;
就着芳草摇曳起舞。
我是情人的礼物;我是婚礼的花环;
我是幸福时刻的记忆;
我是生者给予死者最后的祭献;
我一半是欢乐,一半为忧伤。

但我仰望只看到光明;
从不低头看自己的身影。
这是人必须领会的智慧。

沙与沫 （冰心 译）

1

Trees are poems that the earth writes upon the sky. We fell them down and turn them into paper that we may record our emptiness.

热词天地

turn into （使）变成；译成；成为

树木是大地写上天空中的诗。
我们把它们砍下造纸，
让我们可以把我们的空洞记录下来。

2

The significance of man is not in what he attains, but rather in what he longs to attain[1].

热词天地

1.attain [ə'teɪn] **vt.** 达到，实现；获得；到达
vi. 达到；获得；到达

一个人的意义不在于他的成就，
而在于他所企求成就的东西。

3

Should a tree write its autobiography[1] it would not be unlike the history of a race.

热词天地

1.autobiography [ɔːtəbaɪˈɒɡrəfɪ] **n.** 自传；自传文学

如果一棵树也写自传的话，
它不会不像一个民族的历史。

4

There are three miracles of our Brother Jesus not yet recorded
in the Book:
the first that He was a man like you and me,
the second that He had a sense of humour,
and the third that He knew
He was a conqueror though conquered.

我们的弟兄耶稣还有三桩奇迹没有在经书上记载过:
第一件是他是和你我一样的人;
第二件是他有幽默感;
第三件是他知道他虽然被征服,
而却是一个征服者。

5

Poetry is a deal of joy and pain and wonder, with a dash of the dictionary.

诗是欢乐、痛苦和惊奇穿插着词汇的一场交道。

6

In vain shall a poet seek the mother of the songs of his heart.

一个诗人要想寻找他心里诗歌的母亲的话,是徒劳无功的。

7

Once I said to a poet,
"We shall not know your worth until you die."

And he answered saying, "Yes, death is always the revealer.
And if indeed you would know my worth
it is that I have more in my heart than upon my tongue,
and more in my desire than in my hand."

我曾对一个诗人说：
"不到你死后我们不会知道你的价值。"

他回答说："是的，死亡永远是个揭露者。
如果你真想知道我的价值，
那就是我心里的比舌上的多，
我所愿望的比手里现有的多。"

8

If you sing of beauty though alone in the heart of the desert
 you will have an audience.

如果你歌颂美,
即使你是在沙漠的中心,
你也会有听众。

9

Poetry is wisdom that enchants the heart.
　　Wisdom is poetry that sings in the mind.

　　If we could enchant man's heart and at the same time sing in his mind,
　　　Then in truth he would live in the shadow of God.

诗是迷醉心怀的智慧。
智慧是心思里歌唱的诗。

如果我们能够迷醉人的心怀,
同时也在他的心思中歌唱。
那么他就真的在神的影中生活了。

10

Inspiration will always sing;
inspiration will never explain.

灵感总是歌唱;灵感从不解释。

11

We often sing lullabies to our children
that we ourselves may sleep.

All our words are but crumbs
that fall down from the feast of the mind.

我们常为使自己入睡,
而对我们的孩子唱催眠的歌曲。

我们的一切字句,
都是从心思的筵席上散落下来的残屑。

12

Thinking is always the stumbling stone to poetry.

A great singer is he who sings our silences.

思想对于诗往往是一块绊脚石。

能唱出我们的沉默的,
是一个伟大的歌唱家。

13

How can you sing, If your mouth is filled with food?

How shall your hand be raised in blessing if it is filled with gold?

如果你嘴里含满了食物,你怎能歌唱呢?
如果手里握满金钱,你怎能举起祝福之手呢?

14

They say the nightingale pierces his bosom with a thorn
when he sings his love song.

So do we all.
How else should we sing?

他们说夜莺唱着恋歌的时候,
把刺扎进自己的心膛。

我们也都是这样的。
不这样我们还能歌唱吗?

15

Genius is but a robin's song at the beginning of a slow spring.

天才只不过是晚春开始时节知更鸟所唱的一首歌。

16

Even the most winged spirit cannot escape physical necessity.

连那最高超的心灵,也逃不出物质的需要。

17

Madman is not less a musician than you or myself;

only the instrument on which he plays is a little out of tune.

疯人作为一个音乐家并不比你我逊色;
不过他所弹奏的乐器有点失调而已。

18

The song that lies silent in the heart of a mother sings upon the lips of her child.

在母亲心里沉默着的诗歌,在她孩子的唇上唱了出来。

19

I have never agreed with my other self wholly.
The truth of the matter seems to lie between us.

Your other self is always sorry for you.
But your other self grows on sorrow;
so all is well.

我和另外一个我,从来没有完全一致过。
事物的实质似乎横梗在我们中间。

你的另外一个你总是为你难过。
但是你的另外一个你就在难过中成长;
那么就一切都好了。

20

You are free before the sun of the day, and free before the stars of the night;
And you are free when there is no sun and no moon and no star.
You are even free when you close your eyes upon all there is.

But you are a slave to him whom you love because you love him,
And a slave to him who loves you because he loves you.

你在白天的太阳前面是自由的,在黑夜的星辰前面也是自由的;
在没有太阳,没有月亮,没有星辰的时候,你也是自由的。
就是在你对世上一切闭起眼睛的时候,你也是自由的。

但是你是你所爱的人的奴隶,因为你爱了他。
你也是爱你的人的奴隶,因为他爱了你。

21

There is no struggle of soul and body save in the minds of those whose souls are asleep and whose bodies are out of tune.

除了在那些灵魂熟睡、躯壳失调的人的心里之外,灵魂和躯壳之间是没有斗争的。

22

When you reach the heart of life you shall find beauty in all things,
even in the eyes that are blind to beauty.

当你达到生命的中心的时候,
你将在万物中甚至于在看不见美的人的眼睛里,
也会找到美。

23

Sow a seed and the earth will yield you a flower.

Dream your dream to the sky and it will bring you your beloved.

撒下一粒种子,
大地会给你一朵花。
向天祝愿一个梦想,
天空会给你一个情人。

24

The devil died the very day you were born. Now you do not have to go through hell to meet an angel.

你生下来的那一天,魔鬼就死去了。
你不必经过地狱去会见天使。

25

Many a woman borrows a man's heart;
very few could possess it.

许多女子借到了男子的心;
很少女子能占有它。

26

If you would possess you must not claim.

When a man's hand touches the hand of a woman
they both touch the heart of eternity.

如果你想占有,你千万不可要求。

当一个男子的手接触到一个女子的手,
他俩都接触到了永在的心。

27

Every man loves two women;
the one is the creation of his imagination,
and the other is not yet born.

每一个男子都爱着两个女人：
一个是他想象的作品，
另外一个还没有生下来。

28

Men who do not forgive women their little faults
will never enjoy their great virtues.

不肯原谅女人的细微过失的男子，
永远不会欣赏她们伟大的德性。

29

Love that does not renew itself every day
becomes a habit and in turn a slavery.

不日日自新的爱情,
变成一种习惯,而终于变成奴役。

30

Love and doubt have never been on speaking terms.
Love is a word of light, written by a hand of light, upon a page of light.

恋爱和疑忌是永不交谈的。
爱情是一个光明的字,
被一只光明的手写在一张光明的册页上的。

第四卷

哀·乐

先知 （冰心 译）

On Pain

And a woman spoke, saying, "Tell us of Pain."
And he said:

Your pain is the breaking of the shell that encloses[1] your understanding.
Even as the stone of the fruit must break, that its heart may stand in the sun, so must you know pain.

And could you keep your heart in wonder at the daily miracles[2] of your life, your pain would not seem less wondrous than your joy;
And you would accept the seasons of your heart, even as you have always accepted the seasons that pass over your fields.
And you would watch with serenity[3] through the winters of your grief.

Much of your pain is self-chosen.

It is the bitter potion by which the physician within you heals your sick self.

Therefore trust the physician, and drink his remedy in silence and tranquility[4]:

For his hand, though heavy and hard, is guided by the tender hand of the unseen,

And the cup he brings, though it burn your lips, has been fashioned of the clay which the potter has moistened with his own sacred tears.

热词天地

1.enclose [ɪnˈkləʊz] *vt.* （用墙、篱笆等）把……围起来
2.miracle [ˈmɪrəkl] *n.* 奇迹，圣迹，神迹
3.serenity [səˈrenəti] *n.* 安详；宁静；尊贵的阁下
4.tranquility [trænˈkwɪlɪti] *n.* 平静；安静

苦痛

于是一个妇人说:"请给我们谈苦痛。"

他说:

你的苦痛是你那包裹知识的皮壳的破碎。

连果核也必须破碎,使果仁可以暴露在阳光中,所以你也必须知道苦痛。

倘若你能使你的心时常赞叹日常生活的神妙,你的苦痛的神妙必不减于你的欢乐;

你要承受你心天的季候,如同你常常承受从田野上度过的四时。

你要静守,度过你心里凄凉的冬日。

许多的苦痛是你自择的。

那是你身中的医生,医治你病躯的苦药。

所以你要信托这医生,静默安宁地吃他的药:

因为他的手腕虽重而辣,却是有冥冥的温柔之手指导着,

他带来的药杯,虽会焚灼你的嘴唇,那陶土却是陶工用他自己神圣的眼泪来润湿调抟而成的。

On Pleasure

Then a hermit, who visited the city once a year, came forth and said, "Speak to us of Pleasure."

And he answered, saying:

Pleasure is a freedom song,
But it is not freedom.
It is the blossoming of your desires,
But it is not their fruit.
It is a depth calling unto a height,
But it is not the deep nor the high.
It is the caged taking wing,
But it is not space encompassed[1].
Ay, in very truth, pleasure is a freedom song.
And I fain would have you sing it with fullness of heart; yet I would not have you lose your hearts in the singing.

Some of your youth seek pleasure as if it were all, and they are judged and rebuked[2].

I would not judge nor rebuke them. I would have them seek.

For they shall find pleasure, but not her alone:

Seven are her sisters, and the least of them is more beautiful than pleasure.

Have you not heard of the man who was digging in the earth for roots and found a treasure?

And some of your elders remember pleasures with regret like wrongs committed in drunkenness.

But regret is the beclouding[3] of the mind and not its chastisement[4].

They should remember their pleasures with gratitude, as they would the harvest of a summer.

Yet if it comforts them to regret, let them be comforted.

And there are among you those who are neither young to seek nor old to remember;

And in their fear of seeking and remembering they shun all pleasures, lest they neglect the spirit or offend against it.

But even in their foregoing[5] is their pleasure.

And thus they too find a treasure though they dig for roots with quivering hands.

But tell me, who is he that can offend the spirit?

Shall the nightingale offend the stillness of the night, or the firefly the stars?

And shall your flame or your smoke burden the wind?

Think you the spirit is a still pool which you can trouble with a staff?

Oftentimes in denying yourself pleasure you do but store the desire in the recesses of your being.

Who knows but that which seems omitted today, waits for tomorrow?

Even your body knows its heritage and its rightful need and will not be deceived.

And your body is the harp of your soul,

And it is yours to bring forth sweet music from it or confused sounds.

And now you ask in your heart, "How shall we distinguish that which is good in pleasure from that which is not good?"

Go to your fields and your gardens, and you shall learn that it is the pleasure of the bee to gather honey of the flower,

But it is also the pleasure of the flower to yield its honey to the bee.

For to the bee a flower is a fountain of life,

And to the flower a bee is a messenger of love,

And to both, bee and flower, the giving and the receiving of pleasure is a need and an ecstasy.

People of Orphalese, be in your pleasures like the flowers and the bees.

热词天地

1.encompass [ɪnˈkʌmpəs] *vt.* 围绕，包围；包含或包括某事物
2.rebuke [rɪˈbjuːk] *vt.* 非难，指责；制止，阻止
3.becloud [bɪˈklaʊd] *vt.* 使遮暗，蒙蔽
4.chastisement [ˈtʃæstɪzmənt] *n.* 惩罚
5.foregoing [fɔːˈɡəʊɪŋ] *adj.* 在前的，在先的，前面提到的

逸乐

于是有个每年进城一次的隐士,走上前来说:"给我们谈逸乐。"
他回答说:

逸乐是一阕自由的歌,
却不是自由。
是你的愿望开出的花朵,
却不是结下的果实。
是从深处到高处的招呼,
却不是深,也不是高。
是关闭在笼中的翅翼,
却不是被围绕住的太空。
噫,实话说,逸乐只是一阕自由的歌。
我愿意你们全心全意地歌唱,我却不愿你们在歌唱中迷恋。

你们中间有些年轻的人,寻求逸乐,似乎这便是世上的一切。他们已被裁判、被谴责了。
我不要裁判、谴责他们,我要他们去寻求。
因为他们必会寻到逸乐,但不止找到她一个人:
她有七个姊妹,最小的比逸乐还娇媚。
你们没听见过有人因为要挖掘树根却发现了宝藏么?
你们中间有些老人,想起逸乐时总带些懊悔,如同想起醉中所犯的过失。
然而,懊悔只是心灵的蒙蔽,而不是心灵的惩罚。
你们想起逸乐时应当带着感谢,如同秋收对于夏季的感谢。
但是假如懊悔能予他们以安慰,就让他们得到安慰罢。

你们中间有的不是寻求的青年人,也不是追忆的老年人;
在他们的畏惧寻求与追忆之中,他们远离一切的逸乐,他们深恐疏远了或触犯了心灵。

然而，他们的放弃就是逸乐了。

这样，他们虽用震颤的手挖掘树根，他们也找到宝藏了。

告诉我，谁能触犯心灵呢？

夜莺能触犯静默么，萤火能触犯星辰么？

你们的火焰和烟气能使风感到负载么？

你们认为心灵是一池止水，你能用竿子去搅拨它么？

常常在你拒绝逸乐的时候，你只是把欲望收藏在你心身的隐处。

谁知道在今日似乎避免了的事情，等到明日不会再浮现呢？

连你的身体都知道他的遗传和正当的需要而不肯被欺骗。

你的身体是你灵魂的琴，

无论他发出甜柔的音乐或嘈杂的声响，那都是你的。

现在你们在心中自问："我们如何辨别逸乐中的善与不善呢？"

到你的田野和花园里去，你就知道在花中采蜜是蜜蜂的娱乐；

但是，将蜜汁送给蜜蜂也是花的娱乐。

因为对于蜜蜂，花是它生命的泉源，

对于花，蜜蜂是它恋爱的使者，

对于蜂和花，两下里，娱乐的授受是一种需要与欢乐。

阿法利斯的民众呵，在娱乐中你们应当像花朵与蜜蜂。

On Joy and Sorrow

Then a woman said, "Speak to us of Joy and Sorrow[1]."

And he answered: Your joy is your sorrow unmasked. And the selfsame[2] well from which your laughter rises was oftentimes filled with your tears. And how else can it be? The deeper that sorrow carves into your being, the more joy you can contain. Is not the cup that holds your wine the very cup that was burned in the potter's oven? And is not the lute that soothes[3] your spirit the very wood that was hollowed with knives? When you are joyous, look deep into your heart and you shall find it is only that which has given you sorrow that is giving you joy. When you are sorrowful, look again in your heart, and you shall see that in truth you are weeping for that which has been your delight.

Some of you say, "Joy is greater than sorrow," and others say, "Nay, sorrow is the greater."

But I say unto you, they are inseparable[4]. Together they come, and when one sits alone with you at your board, remember that the other is asleep upon your bed.

Verily you are suspended like scales between your sorrow and your joy. Only when you are empty are you at standstill and balanced. When the treasure-keeper lifts you to weigh his gold and his silver, needs must your joy or your sorrow rise or fall.

热词天地

1. sorrow ['sɒrəʊ] *n.* 悲痛；悔恨，惋惜
2. selfsame ['selfseɪm] *adj.* 完全一样的，相同的
3. soothe [suːð] *vt.* 安慰；缓和；使平静
4. inseparable [ɪn'sepr əbl] *adj.* 不可分的，分不开的；不能分离的

哀乐

于是一个妇人说:"请给我们讲欢乐与悲哀。"

他回答说:

你的欢乐,就是你去了面具的悲哀。

连你那涌溢欢乐的井泉,也常是充满了你的眼泪。

不然又怎样呢?

悲哀的创痕在你身上刻得越深,你越能容受更多的欢乐。

你盛酒的杯,不就是那曾在陶工的窑中燃烧的坯子么?

那感悦你心神的笛子,不就是曾受尖刀挖刻的木管么?

当你欢乐的时候,深深地内顾你的心中,你就知道只不过是曾使你悲哀的,又在使你欢乐。

当你悲哀的时候,再内顾你的心中,你就看出实在是那曾使你喜悦的,又在使你哭泣。

你们有些人说:"欢乐大于悲哀。"也有人说:"不,悲哀是更大的。"

我却要对你们说,它们是不能分开的。

它们一同来到,当这一个和你同席的时候,要记住那一个正在你床上酣眠。

真的,你是天平般悬在悲哀与欢乐之间。

只有在盘空的时候,你才能静止、持平。

当守库者把你提起来称他的金银的时候,你的哀乐就必须升降了。

泪与笑

Yesterday and Today

The gold-hoarder walked in his palace park and with him walked his troubles. And over his head hovered[1] worries as a vulture[2] hovers over a carcass, until he reached a beautiful lake surrounded by magnificent marble statuary.

He sat there pondering the water which poured from the mouths of the statues like thoughts flowing freely from a lover's imagination, and contemplating[3] heavily his palace which stood upon a knoll like a birth-mark upon the cheek of a maiden. His fancy revealed to him the pages of his life's drama which he read with falling tears that veiled his eyes and prevented him from viewing man's feeble additions to Nature.

He looked back with piercing[4] regret to the images of his early life, woven into pattern by the Gods, until he could no longer control his anguish. He said aloud, "Yesterday I was grazing my sheep in the green valley, enjoying my existence, sounding my flute, and holding my head high. Today I am a prisoner of greed. Gold leads into gold, then into restlessness and finally into crushing misery.

"Yesterday I was like a singing bird, soaring freely here and there in the fields. Today I am a slave to fickle wealth, society's rules, and city's customs, and purchased friends, pleasing the people by conforming to the strange and narrow laws of man. I was born to be free and enjoy the bounty of life, but I find myself like a beast of burden so heavily laden with gold that his back is breaking.

"Where are the spacious plains, the singing brooks, the pure breeze, the closeness of Nature? Where is my deity? I have lost all! Naught remains save loneliness that saddens me, gold that ridicules me, slaves who curse to my back, and a palace that I have erected as a tomb for my happiness, and in whose greatness I have lost my heart.

"Yesterday I roamed the prairies and the hills together with the Bedouin's daughter; Virtue was our companion, Love our delight, and the moon our guardian. Today I am among women with shallow beauty who sell themselves for gold and diamonds.

"Yesterday I was carefree, sharing with the shepherds all the joy of life; eating, playing, working, singing, and dancing together to the music of the heart's truth. Today I find myself among the people like a frightened lamb among the wolves. As I walk in the roads, they gaze at me with hateful eyes and point at me with scorn and jealousy, and as I steal through the park I see frowning faces all about me.

"Yesterday I was rich in happiness and today I am poor in gold.

"Yesterday I was a happy shepherd looking upon his head as a merciful king looks with pleasure upon his contented subjects. Today I am a slave standing before my wealth, my wealth which robbed me of the beauty of life I once knew.

"Forgive me, my Judge! I did not know that riches would put my life in fragments and lead me into the dungeons of harshness and stupidity. What I thought was glory is naught but an eternal inferno."

He gathered himself wearily and walked slowly toward the palace, sighing and repeating, "Is this what people call wealth? Is this the God I

am serving and worshipping? Is this what I seek of the earth? Why can I not trade it for one particle of contentment? Who would sell me one beautiful thought for a ton of gold? Who would give me one moment of love for a handful of gems? Who would grant me an eye that can see others' hearts, and take all my coffers in barter?"

As he reached the palace gates he turned and looked toward the city as Jeremiah gazed toward Jerusalem. He raised his arms in woeful lament and shouted, "Oh people of the noisome city, who are living in darkness, hastening toward misery, preaching falsehood, and speaking with stupidity...until when shall you remain ignorant? Unit when shall you abide in the filth of life and continue to desert its gardens? Why wear you tattered robes of narrowness while the silk raiment of Nature's beauty is fashioned for you? The lamp of wisdom is dimming; it is time to furnish it with oil. The house of true fortune is being destroyed; it is time to rebuild it and guard it. The thieves of ignorance have stolen the treasure of your peace; it is time to retake it!"

At that moment a poor man stood before him and stretched forth his hand for alms. As he looked at the beggar, his lips parted, his eyes brightened with a softness, and his face radiated kindness. It was as if the yesterday he had lamented by the lake had come to greet him. He embraced the pauper with affection and filled his hands with gold, and with a voice sincere with the sweetness of love he said, "Come back tomorrow and bring with you your fellow sufferers. All your possessions will be restored."

He entered his palace saying, "Everything in life is good; even gold, for it teaches a lesson. Money is like a stringed instrument; he who does not know how to use it properly will hear only discordant music. Money is like love; it kills slowly and painfully the one who withholds it, and it enlivens the other who turns it upon his fellow man."

热词天地

1. hover ['hɒvə(r)] *vi.* 盘旋；徘徊；犹豫
2. vulture ['vʌltʃə(r)] *n.* 秃鹰，秃鹫；贪婪的人
3. contemplate ['kɒntəmpleɪt] *vt.* 注视，凝视；盘算
4. piercing ['pɪəsɪŋ] *adj.* （指风、寒冷等）刺骨的；（眼睛或眼神）锐利的；锋利的
   reveal to 向……透露
   lead into 把……带入；导致

今与昔

富翁漫步在自己公馆的花园，烦恼如影随形。忧虑在他头上徘徊，似秃鹰在尸体上空盘旋。直到他到了一个被宏伟的大理石雕像环绕的美丽湖泊前。

他坐在那里沉思，那些喷泉自雕像的嘴中倾泻而下，宛若种种思绪在恋人的脑海徜徉；他久久凝思着他那壮丽的公馆，它坐落于那圆丘之上，似少女脸颊上的一块胎记。他幻想翻开并阅读他生命的剧本，读着读着已泪眼迷离，没有看到人类在自然界的无足轻重。

带着钻心的遗憾，他追忆往昔，在上帝设计的模式中成长，然后再也抑制不住痛苦。他大声说道："往昔，我在那绿色的山野放牧群羊，惬意自由，吹响长笛，昂首前进。如今，我成了贪欲的俘虏。被金钱驱使，走向焦虑不安，最后变成彻头彻尾的不幸。

"往昔，我像婉转欢唱的小鸟，在田野中自由地飞来飞去。如今，我成了善变财富和世俗陈规的囚徒：用金钱收买朋友，遵循陌生者的条条框框取悦于人。我本应生来自由，尽享生命之繁盛。可如今，我觉得自己像一只几乎被黄金的重担压垮的野兽。

"如今，那广阔的平原在哪儿？那欢唱的溪流在哪儿？那云淡风清在哪儿？人自然的亲和在哪儿？我的神性又在哪儿？我已失去了这一切。没有什么留下，只剩孤独徒增悲哀，金子笑我荒谬，奴仆在背后咒骂我，我建立的公馆成为我幸福的坟墓，在它的壮伟之中，我已丢失了我的心。

"往昔,我同贝都因人的女儿一起,漫步于草原和山谷之间。美德与我们结伴同行,爱情令我们愉悦,月亮是我们的护卫。如今,我被一群肤浅的美女环绕,她们为了黄金和钻石出卖自己。

"往昔,我无忧无虑,同一群牧羊小伙伴共享生命之欢乐,饮食、嬉戏、工作、唱歌、伴着真实心灵的音乐翩然起舞。如今,我在人们中间好似受到恶狼威胁的小羊羔,心惊胆战:当我走上大街,他们以憎恨的目光盯着我,带着轻蔑和嫉妒对我指指点点;当我偷偷穿过公园,我看到对我皱眉的面孔比比皆是。

"往昔,我是拥有幸福的大富翁;如今,我是只拥有金钱的可怜虫。

"往昔,我是仰望苍穹的一个快乐牧童,正如仁慈的国王愉悦地看着他满意的臣民;如今,我沦为呆站在财富之前的奴隶,而这财富夺走了我曾经熟识的生命的美好。

"宽恕我吧,上帝!我不知财富会将我的生活变得支离破碎,将我引向那粗糙和愚昧的地牢。我也不知道众人追逐的荣耀竟成为永恒的地狱。"

富翁无力地站起,缓缓地走向他的公馆,不断地轻叹并重复着:"难道这就是人们所谓的'财富'吗?这就是我情愿服侍并崇拜的上帝吗?这就是我终尽一生要追寻的东西吗?为什么用它买不来一丝一毫的满足?谁愿意卖给我价值一吨黄金的美好思想?谁愿意用一把珠宝卖给我一瞬的爱情?谁愿意拿走我的金仓银库,给我一只能够看清众人内心的眼睛?"

当他抵达公馆门口时,他转身,远望着这座城市,犹如当年耶利米凝视着耶路撒冷,他在悲哀的悼歌中举起手臂,大声喊道:"生活在有害城市中的人们呀,你们在黑暗中生活、急切地奔向悲惨、颠倒是非、胡说八道,你们的愚昧无知要到何时?你们抛弃生命的花园,忍受生活的污浊要到何时?美丽的大自然明明为你们准备了绫罗绸缎,你们为何要披上狭隘的破衣烂衫?智慧之灯已经渐次暗淡,是时候将它添油擦亮了!你真正财富的庄园已被损毁,是时候重建和守卫了!无知的盗贼已窃取了你宝贵的安宁,是时候将它拿回来了!"

就在此时,一个穷人站在他面前,向他伸出乞讨之手。富翁瞧着这个乞讨之人,嘴唇微微颤动,眼睛流动出温柔的光彩,脸庞闪耀着和蔼的光辉。犹如他方才在湖畔悼念的往昔向他致以问候了。他深情地给了乞丐一个拥抱,在他手心塞满金币,以充满真诚和怜爱的声音对他说道:"明天你再过来,领着你的受苦难的同伴们一起来。你们所有的财产都将被恢复。"

富翁走进了公馆,说道:"人生的一切都是美好的,甚至包括金钱,因为它会给人以教益。金钱犹如一种弦乐器,不会正确弹奏的人,只能听到它刺耳的噪音。金钱又犹如爱情,抓牢它的人,会被它缓慢而痛苦地杀死;慷慨地将它给予同伴的人,它会使他得到再生。"

沙与沫 (冰心 译)

1

Do not the spirits who dwell¹ in the ether envy man his pain?

热词天地

1.dwell [dwel] *vi.* 居住；存在于；细想某事

难道在以太里居住的精灵，不妒羡世人的痛苦吗？

2

How can I lose faith in the justice of life,
when the dreams of those who sleep upon feathers are not more beautiful
than the dreams of those who sleep upon the earth?

当那些睡在绒毛上面的人所做的梦,
并不比睡在土地上的人的梦更美好的时候,
我怎能对生命的公平失掉信心呢?

3

If there is such a thing as sin some of us commit it backward following our forefathers' footsteps;

And some of us commit it forward by overruling our children.

如果真的存在罪孽,
我们中一些人将沿着先祖的足迹重复罪过;

另一些人则将因否决我们的孩子而再次犯错。

4

Lovers embrace that which is between them rather than each other.

情人只拥抱了他们之间的一种东西,而没有互相拥抱。

5

Friendship is always a sweet responsibility, never an opportunity.

If you do not understand your friend under all conditions
you will never understand him.

友谊永远是一个甜柔的责任,
从来不是一种机会。

如果你不在所有的情况下了解你的朋友,
你就永远不会了解他。

6

If you would rise but a cubit above race and country and self
you would indeed become godlike.

只要你从种族、国家和自身之上,
升起一腕尺,
你就真成了神一样的人。

7

You are but a fragment of your giant self,
a mouth that seeks bread,
and a blind hand that holds the cup for a thirsty mouth.

你不过是你的大我的一个碎片,
一张寻求面包的嘴,
一只盲目的、为一张干渴的嘴举着水杯的手。

8

Your most radiant garment is of the other person's weaving;

You most savory meal is that which you eat at the other person's table;

Your most comfortable bed is in the other person's house.

Now tell me, how can you separate yourself from the other person?

你的最华丽的衣袍是别人织造的；

你的最可口的一餐是在别人的桌上吃的；

你的最舒适的床铺是在别人的房子里的。

那么请告诉我，你怎能把自己同别人分开呢？

9

Your mind and my heart will never agree
until your mind ceases to live in numbers
and my heart in the mist.

你的心思和我的心怀将永远不会一致,

除非你的心思不再居留于数字中,而我的心怀不再居留在云雾里。

10

We shall never understand one another until we reduce the language to seven words.

除非我们把语言减少到七个字,我们将永不会互相了解。

11

Only great sorrow or great joy can reveal your truth.

If you would be revealed you must either dance naked in the sun, or carry your cross.

只有深哀和极乐才能显露你的真实。
如果你愿意被显露出来，
你必须在阳光中裸舞，或是背起你的十字架。

12

You see but your shadow when you turn your back to the sun.

当你背向太阳的时候，你只看到自己的影子。

13

Should Nature heed what we say of contentment no river would seek the sea,
and no winter would turn to Spring.
Should she heed all we say of thrift,
how many of us would be breathing this air?

如果自然听到了我们所说的知足的话语，
江河就不去寻求大海，
冬天就不会变成春天。
如果她听到我们所说的一切吝啬的话语，
我们有多少人可以呼吸到空气呢？

14

We are all beggars at the gate of the temple,
and each one of us receives his share of the bounty of the King when he enters the temple, and when he goes out.
But we are all jealous of one another,
which is another way of belittling the King.

我们都是庙门前的乞丐，当国王进出庙门的时候，我们每人都分受到恩赏。
但是我们都互相妒忌，这是轻视国王的另一种方式。

15

If it were not for your guests all houses would be graves.

如果不为待客的话,所有的房屋都成了坟墓。

16

Said a gracious wolf to a simple sheep,
"Will you not honor our house with a visit?"

And the sheep answered,
"We would have been honored to visit your house if it were not in your stomach."

和善的狼对天真的羊说:"你不光临寒舍吗?"
羊回答说:"我们将以到访贵府为荣,如果贵府不是在你肚子里的话。"

17

You cannot consume beyond your appetite.
The other half of the loaf belongs to the other person,
and there should remain a little bread for the chance guest.

你不能吃得多过你的食欲。
那一半食粮是属于别人的,
而且也还要为不速之客留下一点面包。

18

I stopped my guest on the threshold and said,
"Nay, wipe not your feet as you enter, but as you go out."

Generosity is not in giving me that which I need more than you do,
but it is in giving me that which you need more than I do.

我把客人拦在门口说：
"不必了，在出门的时候再擦脚吧，进门的时候是不必擦的。"

慷慨不是你把我比你更需要的东西给我，
而是你把你比我更需要的东西也给了我。

19

You are indeed charitable when you give,
and while giving, turn your face away
so that you may not see the shyness of the receiver.

当你施与的时候你当然是慈善的，
在授与的时候要把脸转过一边，
这样就可以不看那受者的羞赧。

20

The difference between the richest man and the poorest is
but a day of hunger and an hour of thirst.

最富与最穷的人的差别，
只在于一整天的饥饿和一个钟头的干渴。

21

I too am visited by angels and devils, but I get rid of them.

When it is an angel I pray an old prayer, and he is bored;
When it is a devil I commit an old sin, and he passes me by.

我也曾受过天使和魔鬼的造访,但是我都把他们支走了。

当天使来的时候,我念一段旧的诗文,他就厌烦了;
当魔鬼来的时候,我犯一次旧的罪过,他就从我面前走过了。

22

After all this is not a bad prison;
but I do not like this wall between my cell and the next prisoner's cell;

Yet I assure you that I do not wish to reproach the warder not the builder of the prison.

总的说来,
这不是一所坏监狱;
我只不喜欢在我的囚房和隔壁囚房之间的这堵墙;
但是我对你保证,
我决不愿责备狱吏和建造这监狱的人。

23

Trickery succeeds sometimes, but it always commits suicide.

欺骗有时成功,但它往往自杀。

24

You are truly a forgiver when you forgive murderers who never spill blood,
thieves who never steal, and liars who utter no falsehood.

当你饶恕那些从不流血的凶手,
从不窃盗的小偷,不打禅语的说谎者的时候,
你就真是一个宽大的人。

25

If your heart is a volcano how shall you expect flowers to bloom in your hands?

如果你的心是一座火山的话,
你怎能指望会从你的手里开出花朵来呢?

26

He who can put his finger upon that which divides good from evil is he who can touch the very hem of the garment of God.

谁能把手指放在善恶分野的地方,
谁就是能够摸到上帝圣袍的边缘的人。

27

A strange form of self-indulgence!
There are times when I would be wronged and cheated,
that I may laugh at the expense of those
who think I do not know I am being wronged and cheated.

多么奇怪的一个自欺的方式!
有时我宁愿受到损害和欺骗,
好让我嘲笑那些以为我不知道我是被损害、欺骗了的人。

28

What shall I say of him who is the pursuer playing the part of the pursued?

对于一个扮作被追求者的角色的追求者,我该怎么说他呢?

29

Let him who wipes his soiled hands with your garment take your garment.
He may need it again; surely you would not.

让那个把脏手在你衣服上擦的人,
把你的衣服拿走吧。
他也许还需要那件衣服,
你却一定不会再要了。

30

It is a pity that money-changers cannot be good gardeners.

兑换商不能做一个好园丁,真是可惜。

31

Please do not whitewash your inherent faults with your acquired virtues.
I would have the faults; they are like mine own.

请你不要以后天的德行来粉饰你先天的缺陷。
我宁愿有缺陷;
这些缺陷和我自己的一样。

32

Even the masks of life are masks of deeper mystery.
You may judge others only according to your knowledge of yourself.

Tell me now, who among us is guilty and who is unguilty?
The truly just is he who feels half guilty of your misdeeds.

就是生命的面具也都是更深的奥秘的面具。
你可能只根据自己的了解去判断别人。

现在告诉我,我们里头谁是有罪的,谁是无辜的?
真正公平的人就是对你的罪过感到应该分担的人。

33

How often have I attributed to myself crimes I have never committed,
so that the other person may feel comfortable in my presence.

有多少次我把没有犯过的罪都拉到自己身上,为的让人家在我面前感到舒服。

34

Only an idiot and a genius break man-made laws;
and they are the nearest to the heart of God.

只有白痴和天才,才会去破坏人造的法律;
他们离上帝的心最近。

35

It is only when you are pursued that you become swift.

只在你被追逐的时候,你才快跑。

36

I have no enemies, O God, but if I am to have an enemy
Let his strength be equal to mine,
That truth alone may be the victor.

我没有仇人,上帝呵!如果我会有仇人的话,
就让他和我势均力敌,
只让真理做一个战胜者。

37

Long ago there lived a Man who was crucified for being too loving and too lovable.
And strange to relate I met him thrice yesterday.

The first time He was asking a policeman not to take a prostitute to prison; the second time He was drinking wine with an outcast; and the third time He was having a fist-fight with a promoter inside a church.

If all they say of good and evil were true, then my life is but one long crime.

很久以前一个"人",因为过于爱别人,也因太可爱了,而被钉在十字架上。说来奇怪,昨天我碰到他三次。

第一次是他恳求一个警察不要把一个妓女关到监牢里去;第二次是他和一个无赖一块喝酒;第三次是他在教堂里和一个法官拳斗。

如果他们所谈的善恶都是正确的话,那么我的一生只是一个长时间的犯罪。

38

You will be quite friendly with your enemy when you both die.

当你和敌人都死了的时候,你就会和他十分友好了。

39

Perhaps a man may commit suicide in self-defense.

一个人在自卫的时候可能自杀。

40

Oftentimes I have hated in self-defense; but if I were stronger I would not have used such a weapon.

在自卫中我常常憎恨；但是如果我是一个比较坚强的人，我就不必使用这样的武器。

41

How stupid is he who would patch the hatred in his eyes with the smile of his lips.

把唇上的微笑来遮掩眼里的憎恨的人，是多么愚蠢呵！

42

The only one who has been unjust to me is the one to whose brother I have been unjust.

When you see a man led to prison say in your heart, "Mayhap he is escaping from a narrower prison."

And when you see a man drunken say in your heart, "Mayhap he sought escape from something still more unbeautiful."

过去唯一对我不公平的人，就是那个我曾对他的兄弟不公平的人。

当你看见一个人被带进监狱的时候，在你心中默默地说："也许他是从更狭小的监狱里逃出来的。"

当你看见一个人喝醉了的时候，在你心中默默地说："也许他想躲避某些更不美好的事物。"

43

Only those beneath me can envy or hate me.
I have never been envied nor hated; I am above no one.

Only those above me can praise or belittle me.
I have never been praised nor belittled; I am below no one.

只有在我以下的人,能忌妒我或憎恨我。
我从来没有被妒忌或被憎恨过,我不在任何人之上。

只有在我以上的人,能称赞我或轻蔑我。
我从来没有被称赞或被轻蔑过,我不在任何人之下。

44

Your saying to me, "I do not understand you,"
is praise beyond my worth, and an insult you do not deserve.

How mean am I when life gives me gold and I give you silver,
and yet I deem myself generous.

你对我说：“我不了解你”，
这就是过分地赞扬了我，无故地侮辱了你。

当生命给我金子而我给你银子的时候，
我还自以为慷慨，这是多么卑鄙呵！

45

When you reach the heart of life you will find yourself not higher than the felon,
and not lower than the prophet.

Strange that you should pity the slow-footed and not the slow-minded,
And the blind-eyed rather than the blind-hearted.

当你达到生命心中的时候,
你会发现你不高过罪人,也不低于先知。

奇怪的是,
你竟可怜那脚下慢的人,而不可怜那心里慢的人。
可怜那盲于目的人,而不可怜那盲于心的人。

46

It is wiser for the lame not to break his crutches upon the head of his enemy.

瘸子不在他敌人的头上敲断他的拐杖，是更聪明些的。

47

How blind is he who gives you out of his pocketthat he may take out of your heart

那个认为从他的口袋里给你，
可以从你心里取回的人，是多么糊涂呵!

48

Strange that we all defend our wrongs with more vigor than we do our rights.

Should we all confess our sins to one another we would all laugh at one another for our lack of originality.

Should we all reveal our virtues we would also laugh for the same cause.

奇怪的是,
当我们为错误辩护的时候,
我们用的气力比我们捍卫正确时还大。

如果我们互相供认彼此的罪过的话,
我们就会为大家并无新创而互相嘲笑。
如果我们都公开了我们的美德的话,
我们也将为大家并无新创而大笑。

49

If there is such a thing as sin some of us commit it backward
following our forefathers footsteps;

And some of us commit it forward by overruling our children.

如果世上真有罪孽这件东西的话,
我们中间有的人是跟着我们祖先的脚踪,
倒退着造孽。

有的人是管制着我们的儿女,
赶前地造挚。

50

The truly good is he who is one with all those who are deemed bad.

真正的好人,是那个和所有的大家认为坏的人在一起的人。

51

We are all prisoners
but some of us are in cells with windows
and some without.

我们都是囚犯,
不过有的是关在有窗的牢房里,
有的就关在无窗的牢房里。

52

An individual is above man-made laws
until he commits a crime against man-made conventions;
After that he is neither above anyone nor lower than anyone.

一个人是在人造的法律之上,
直到他犯了抵触人造的惯例的罪;
在此以后,
他就不在任何人之上,
也不在任何人之下。

53

Is there a greater fault than being conscious of the other
person's faults?

还有比意识到别人的过失还大的过
失吗?

54

How heedless you are when you would have men fly
With Your wings and you cannot even give them
a feather.

你要人们用你的翅翼飞翔而却连一根羽毛也拿不出
的时候,
你是多么轻率呵。

55

If the other person laughs at you,
you can pity him;
but if you laugh at him you may never forgive yourself.

If the other person injures you,
you may forget the injury;
but if you injure him you will always remember.

In truth the other person is your most sensitive self given another body.

如果别人嘲笑你,
你可以怜悯他;
但是如果你嘲笑他,
你决不可自恕。

如果别人伤害你,
你可以忘掉它;
但是如果你伤害了他,
你须永远记住。

实际上别人就是最敏感的你,附托在另一个躯壳上。

56

Once a man sat at my board
and ate my bread and drank my wine
and went away laughing at me.

Then he came again for bread and wine,
and I spurned him;
And the angels laughed at me.

从前有人坐在我的桌上,
吃我的饭,喝我的酒,
走时还嘲笑我。

以后他再来要吃要喝,我不理他;
天使就嘲笑我。

57

It is the honor of the murdered that he is not the murderer.

被杀者的光荣就是他不是凶手。

58

Government is an agreement between you and myself.
You and myself are often wrong.

政府是你和我之间的协定。
你和我常常是错误的。

59

Crime is either another name of need or an aspect of a disease.

罪恶是需要的别名,或是疾病的一种。

60

Hate is a dead thing.
Who of you would be a tomb？

憎恨是一件死东西，
你们有谁愿意做一座坟墓？

61

The tribune of humanity is in its silent heart never its talkative Mind.

人道的保护者是在它沉默的心怀中，
从不在它多言的心思里。

62

The most pitiful among men is he who turns his dreams into silver and gold.

We are all climbing toward the summit of our hearts'desire.
Should the other climber steal your sack and your purse and wax fat on the one and heavy on the other, you should pity him;
The climbing will be harder for his flesh, and the burden will make his way longer.

And should you in your leanness see his flesh puffing upward, help him a step; it will add to your swiftness.

最可怜的人是把他的梦想变成金银的人。

我们都在攀登自己心愿的高峰。如果另一个登山者偷了你的粮袋和钱包,而把粮袋装满了,钱包也加重了,你应当可怜他。这攀登将为他的肉体增加困难,这负担将加长他的路程。

如果在你消瘦的情况下,看到他的肉体膨胀着往上爬,帮他一步。这样做会增加你的速度。

63

They deem me mad because I will not sell my days for gold;

And I deem them mad because they think my days have a price.

他们认为我疯了,
因为我不肯拿我的光阴去换金钱;

我认为他们是疯了,
因为他们以为我的光阴是可以估价的。

64

I would not be the least among men with dreams and the desire to fulfill them, rather than the greatest with no dreams and no desires.

我宁可做人类中有梦想和有完成梦想的愿望的、最渺小的人,
而不愿做一个最伟大的、无梦想、无愿望的人。

65

They spread before us their riches of gold and silver, of ivory and ebony,
and we spread before them our hearts and our spirits;

And yet they deem themselves the hosts and us the guests.

他们把最昂贵的金子、银子、象牙和黑檀排列在我们的面前，
我们把心胸和气魄排列在他们的面前；

而他们却自称为主人，把我们当做客人。

第五卷 是·非

先知 （冰心 译）

On Good and Evil

And one of the elders of the city said, "Speak to us of Good and Evil."
And he answered:

Of the good in you I can speak, but not of the evil.
For what is evil but good tortured by its own hunger and thirst?
Verily when good is hungry it seeks food even in dark caves, and when it thirsts, it drinks even of dead waters.

You are good when you are one with yourself.
Yet when you are not one with yourself you are not evil.
For a divided house is not a den[1] of thieves; it is only a divided house.
And a ship without rudder[2] may wander aimlessly among perilous isles yet sink not to the bottom.

You are good when you strive to give of yourself.

Yet you are not evil when you seek gain for yourself.

For when you strive for gain you are but a root that clings to the earth and sucks at her breast.

Surely the fruit cannot say to the root, "Be like me, ripe and full and ever giving of your abundance."

For to the fruit giving is a need, as receiving is a need to the root.

You are good when you are fully awake in your speech,

Yet you are not evil when you sleep while your tongue staggers[3] without purpose.

And even stumbling speech may strengthen a weak tongue.

You are good when you walk to your goal firmly and with bold steps.

Yet you are not evil when you go thither limping[4].

Even those who limp go not backward.

But you who are strong and swift, see that you do not limp before the lame, deeming it kindness.

You are good in countless ways, and you are not evil when you are not good,

You are only loitering and sluggard.

Pity that the stags cannot teach swiftness to the turtles.

In your longing for your giant self lies your goodness: and that longing is in all of you.

But in some of you that longing is a torrent rushing with might to the sea, carrying the secrets of the hillsides and the songs of the forest.

And in others it is a flat stream that loses itself in angles and bends and lingers before it reaches the shore.

But let not him who longs much say to him who longs little, "Wherefore are you slow and halting?"

For the truly good ask not the naked, "Where is your garment?" nor the houseless, "What has befallen your house?"

热词天地

1. den [den] *n.* 兽穴；贼窝；简陋污秽的小室；书斋
2. rudder ['rʌdə(r)] *n.* 船舵；[航] 方向舵
3. stagger ['stæɡə(r)] *vi.* 蹒跚；犹豫；动摇
4. limp [lɪmp] *vi.* 一瘸一拐地走；困难地航行

    strive to 力图，力求

善恶

于是一位城中的长老说:"请给我们谈你们的善恶。"
他回答说:

我能谈你们的善性,却不能谈恶性。
因为,什么是"恶",不只是"善"被他自身的饥渴所困苦么?
的确,在"善"饥饿的时候,他肯向黑洞中觅食,渴的时候,他也肯喝死水。

当你与自己合一的时候便是"善"。
当你不与自己合一的时候,却也不是"恶"。
因为一个隔断的院宇,不是贼窝,只不过是个隔断的院宇。
一只船失了舵,许会在礁岛间无目的地飘荡而却不至于沉到海底。
当你努力要牺牲自己的时候便是"善"。
当你想法自利的时候,却也不是"恶"。
因为当你设法自利的时候,你不过是土里的树根,在大地的胸怀中啜吸。
果实自然不能对树根说:"你要像我,丰满成熟,永远贡献出你最丰满的一部分。"
因为,在果实,贡献是必需的,正如吸收是树根所必需的一样。

当你在言谈中完全清醒的时候,你是"善"的。
当你在睡梦中,舌头无意识地摆动的时候,却也不是"恶"。
连那失错的言语,有时也能激动柔弱的舌头。

当你勇敢地走向目标的时候,你是"善"的。
你颠顿而行,却也不是"恶"。
连那些跛者,也不倒行。
但你们这些勇健而迅速的人,要警醒,不要在跛者面前颠顿,还自以为仁慈。

在无数的事上,你是"善"的;在你不善的时候,你也不是"恶"。
你只是流连,荒亡。
可怜那糜鹿不能教给龟鳖快跑。

在你冀求你的"大我"的时候,便隐存着你的善性:这种冀求是你们每人心中都有的。
但是对于有的人,这种冀求是奔越归海的急湍,挟带着山野的神秘与林木的讴歌。
在其他的人,是在转弯曲折中迷途的缓流的溪水,在归海的路上滞留。
但是不要让那些冀求深的人,对冀求浅的人说:"你为什么这般迟钝?"
因为那真善的人,不问赤裸的人:"你的衣服在那里?"也不问那无家的人:"你的房子怎样了?"

On Crime and Punishment

Then one of the judges of the city stood forth and said, "Speak to us of Crime and Punishment."

And he answered, saying:

It is when your spirit goes wandering upon the wind,

That you, alone and unguarded, commit[1] a wrong unto others and therefore unto yourself.

And for that wrong committed must you knock and wait a while unheeded at the gate of the blessed.

Like the ocean is your god-self,

It remains for ever undefiled[2].

And like the ether it lifts but the winged.

Even like the sun is your god-self,

It knows not the ways of the mole nor seeks It the holes of the serpent.

But your god-self does not dwell[3] alone in your being.

Much in you is still man, and much in you is not yet man,

But a shapeless pigmy that walks asleep in the mist searching for its own awakening.

And of the man in you would I now speak,

For it is he and not your god-self nor the pigmy in the mist[4], that knows crime and the punishment of crime.

Oftentimes have I heard you speak of one who commits a wrong as though he were not one of you, but a stranger unto you and an intruder[5] upon your world.

But I say that even as the holy and the righteous cannot rise beyond the highest which is in each one of you,

So the wicked and the weak cannot fall lower than the lowest which is in you also.

And as a single leaf turns not yellow but with the silent knowledge of the whole tree.

So the wrong-doer cannot do wrong without the hidden will of you all.

Like a procession you walk together towards your god-self.

You are the way and the wayfarers[6].

And when one of you falls down he falls for those behind him, a caution against the stumbling stone.

Ay, and he falls for those ahead of him, who though faster and surer of foot, yet removed not the stumbling stone.

And this also, though the word lie heavy upon your hearts:
The murdered is not unaccountable for his own murder,
And the robbed is not blameless in being robbed.
The righteous is not innocent of the deeds of the wicked,
And the white-handed is not clean in the doings of the felon.
Yea, the guilty is oftentimes the victim of the injured,

And still more often the condemned is the burden bearer for the guiltless and unblamed.

You cannot separate the just from the unjust and the good from the wicked;

For they stand together before the face of the sun even as the black thread and the white are woven together.

And when the black thread breaks, the weaver shall look into the whole cloth, and he shall examine the loom also.

If any of you would bring judgment to the unfaithful wife,
Let him also weight the heart of her husband in scales, and measure his soul with measurements.

And let him who would lash the offender look unto the spirit of the offended.

And if any of you would punish in the name of righteousness and lay the axe unto the evil tree, let him see to its roots;

And verily he will find the roots of the good and the bad, the fruitful and the fruitless, all entwined together in the silent heart of the earth.

And you judges who would be just,

What judgment pronounce you upon him who though honest in the flesh yet is a thief in spirit?

What penalty lay you upon him who slays in the flesh yet is himself slain in the spirit?

And how prosecute you him who in action is a deceiver and an oppressor,

Yet who also is aggrieved and outraged?

And how shall you punish those whose remorse is already greater than their misdeeds?

Is not remorse the justice which is administered by that very law which you would fain serve?

Yet you cannot lay remorse upon the innocent nor lift it from the heart of the guilty.

Unbidden shall it call in the night, that men may wake and gaze upon themselves.

And you who would understand justice, how shall you unless you look upon all deeds in the fullness of light?

Only then shall you know that the erect and the fallen are but one man standing in twilight between the night of his pigmy-self and the day of his god-self,

And that the corner-stone of the temple is not higher than the lowest stone in its foundation.

热词天地

1. commit [kəˈmɪt] *vt.* 犯罪，做错事；把……托付给
2. undefiled [ˌʌndɪˈfaɪld] *adj.* 无污的，洁净的，纯粹的
3. dwell [dwel] *vi.* 居住；存在于；细想某事
4. mist [mɪst] *n.* 薄雾；视线模糊不清
5. intruder [ɪnˈtruːdə(r)] *n.* 闯入者，侵入者；
6. wayfarer [ˈweɪfeərə(r)] *n.* 旅人，（尤指）徒步旅行者

罪与罚

于是本城的法官中,有一个走上前来说:"请给我们谈罪与罚。"
他回答说:

当你的灵性随风飘荡的时候,
你孤零而失慎地对别人也就是对自己犯了过错。
为着所犯的过错,你必须去叩那受福者之门,要被怠慢地等待片刻。

你们的"神性"像海洋;
他永远纯洁不染,
又像以太,他只帮助有翼者上升。
他们的"神性"也像太阳;
他不知道田鼠的径路,也不寻找蛇虺的洞穴。
但是你们的"神性",不是独居在你们里面。
在你们里面,有些仍是"人性",有些还不成"人性"。
只是一个未成形的侏儒,睡梦中在烟雾里蹒跚,自求觉醒。

我现在所要说的,就是你们的"人性"。

因为那知道罪与罪的刑罚的,是他,而不是你的"神性",也不是烟雾中的侏儒。

我常听见你们论议到一个犯了过失的人,仿佛他不是你们的同人,只像是个外人,是个你们的世界中的闯入者。

我却要说,连那圣洁和正直的,也不能高于你们每人心中的至善。

所以那奸邪和懦弱的,也不能低于你们心中的极恶。

如同一片树叶,除非得到全树的默许,不能独自变黄。

所以那作恶者,若没有你们大家无形中的怂恿,也不会作恶。

如同一个队伍,你们一同向着你们的"神性"前进。

你们是道,也是行道的人。

当你们中间有人跌倒的时候,他是为了他后面的人而跌倒,是一块绊脚石的警告。

是的,他也为他前面的人而跌倒,因为他们的步履虽然又快又稳,却没有把那绊脚石挪开。

还有这个,虽然这些话会重压你的心:

被杀者对于自己的被杀不能不负咎,

被劫者对于自己的被劫不能不受责。

正直的人，对于恶人的行为，也不能算无辜。

清白的人，对于罪人的过犯，也不能算不染。

是的，罪犯往往是被害者的牺牲品，

刑徒更往往为那些无罪无过的人担负罪责。

你们不能把至公与不公，至善与不善分开；

因为他们一齐站在太阳面前，如同织在一起的黑线和白线，

黑线断了的时候，织工就要视察整块的布，也要察看那机杼。

你们中如有人要审判一个不忠诚的妻子，

让他也拿天平来称一称她丈夫的心，拿尺来量一量他的灵魂。

让鞭挞"扰人者"的人，先察一察那"被扰者"的灵性。

你们如有人要以正义之名，砍伐一棵恶树，让他先察看树根；

他一定能看出那好的与坏的，能结实与不能结实的树根，都在大地的沉默的心中，纠结在一处。

你们这些愿持公正的法官，

你们将怎样裁判那忠诚其外而盗窃其中的人？

你们又将怎样刑罚一个受戮肉体，而在他自己是心灵遭灭的人？

你们又将怎样控告那行为上刁猾、暴戾，

而事实上也是被威逼、被虐待的人呢？

你们又将怎样责罚那悔心已经大于过失的人？

忏悔不就是你们所喜欢奉行的法定的公道么？

然而你们却不能将忏悔放在无辜者的身上，也不能将它从罪人心中取出。

不期然地它要在夜中呼唤，使人们醒起，反躬自省。

你们这些愿意了解公道的人，若不在大光明中视察一切的行为，你们怎能了解呢？

只在那时，你们才知道那直立与跌倒的，只是一个站在侏儒性的黑夜与神性的白日的黄昏中的人，

也要知道那大殿的角石，也不高于那最低的基石。

On Freedom

And an orator[1] said, "Speak to us of Freedom."
And he answered:

At the city gate and by your fireside I have seen you prostrate[2] yourself and worship your own freedom,

Even as slaves humble themselves before a tyrant and praise him though he slays[3] them.

Ay, in the grove of the temple and in the shadow of the citadel I have seen the freest among you wear their freedom as a yoke and a handcuff.

And my heart bled within me; for you can only be free when even the desire of seeking freedom becomes a harness to you, and when you cease to speak of freedom as a goal and a fulfillment.

You shall be free indeed when your days are not without a care nor your nights without a want and a grief,

But rather when these things girdle your life and yet you rise above them naked and unbound.

And how shall you rise beyond your days and nights unless you break the chains which you at the dawn of your understanding have fastened around your noon hour?

In truth that which you call freedom is the strongest of these chains, though its links glitter in the sun and dazzle[4] your eyes.

And what is it but fragments of your own self you would discard that you may become free?

If it is an unjust law you would abolish[5], that law was written with your own hand upon your own forehead.

You cannot erase it by burning your law books nor by washing the foreheads of your judges, though you pour the sea upon them.

And if it is a despot you would dethrone, see first that his throne erected within you is destroyed.

For how can a tyrant rule the free and the proud, but for a tyranny in their own freedom and a shame in their won pride?

And if it is a care you would cast off, that care has been chosen by you rather than imposed upon you.

And if it is a fear you would dispel, the seat of that fear is in your heart and not in the hand of the feared.

Verily all things move within your being in constant half embrace, the desired and the dreaded, the repugnant[6] and the cherished, the pursued and that which you would escape.

These things move within you as lights and shadows in pairs that cling.

And when the shadow fades and is no more, the light that lingers becomes a shadow to another light.

And thus your freedom when it loses its fetters becomes itself the fetter[7] of a greater freedom.

热词天地

1. orator ['ɒrətə(r)] *n.* 演说者,演讲家
2. prostrate ['prɒstreɪt] *vt.* 使俯伏,使拜倒
3. slay [sleɪ] *vt.* 残杀
4. dazzle ['dæzl] *vt.* 使目眩;使惊异不已
5. abolish [ə'bɒlɪʃ] *vt.* 废除,废止;取消,革除
6. repugnant [rɪ'pʌgnənt] *adj.* 令人厌恶的;矛盾的
7. fetter ['fetə(r)] *n.* 脚镣,束缚

自由

于是一个辩士说:"请给我们谈自由。"
他回答说:

在城门边,在炉火光前,我曾看见你们俯伏敬拜自己的"自由",就像那些囚奴,在诛戮他们的暴君之前卑屈,颂赞。

噫,在庙宇的林中,在城堡的影里,我曾看见你们之中最自由者,把自由像枷铐似地戴上。

我心里忧伤;因为只有那求自由的愿望也成了羁饰,你们再不以自由为标竿、为成就的时候,你们才是自由了。

当你们的白日不是没有牵挂,你们的黑夜也不是没有愿望与忧愁的时候,你们才是自由的。

不如说是当那些事物包围住你的生命,而你却能赤裸地无牵挂地超脱的时候,你们才是自由了。

但若不是在你们了解的晓光中,折断了捆绑你们朝气的锁链,你们怎能超脱你们的白日和黑夜呢?

实话说,你们所谓的自由,就是最坚牢的锁链,虽然那链环闪烁在日光中,炫耀了你们的眼目。

"自由"岂不是你们自身的碎片,你们愿意将它抛弃换得自由么?

假如那是你们所要废除的一条不公平的法律,那法律却是你们用自己的手写在自己的额上的。

你们虽烧毁你们的律书,倾全海的水来冲洗你们法官的额,也不能把它抹掉。

假如那是个你们所要废黜的暴君,先看他建立在你心中的宝座是否毁坏。

因为一个暴君怎能辖制自由和自尊的人呢?除非他们自己的自由是专制的,他们的自尊是可羞的。

假如那是一种你们所要抛掷的牵挂,那牵挂是你自取的,不是别人勉强给你的。

假如那是一种你们所要消灭的恐怖,那恐怖的座位是在你的心中,而不在你所恐怖的人的手里。

真的,一切在你里面运行的事物,愿望与恐怖,憎恶与爱怜,追求与退避,都是永恒地互抱着。

这些事物在你里面运行,如同光明与黑影成对地胶粘着。

当黑影消灭的时候,遗留的光明又变成另一种光明的黑影。

这样,当你们的自由脱去它的镣铐的时候,它本身又变成更大的自由的镣铐了。

On Laws

Then a lawyer said, "But what of our Laws, master?"
And he answered:

You delight in laying down laws,

Yet you delight more in breaking them.

Like children playing by the ocean who build sand-towers with constancy[1] and then destroy them with laughter.

But while you build your sand-towers the ocean brings more sand to the shore,

And when you destroy them, the ocean laughs with you.

Verily[2] the ocean laughs always with the innocent.

But what of those to whom life is not an ocean, and man-made laws are not sand-towers,

But to whom life is a rock, and the law a chisel with which they would carve it in their own likeness?

What of the cripple who hates dancers?

What of the ox who loves his yoke and deems[3] the elk and deer of the forest stray and vagrant[4] things?

What of the old serpent who cannot shed his skin, and calls all others naked and shameless?

And of him who comes early to the wedding-feast, and when over-fed and tired goes his way saying that all feasts[5] are violation and all feasters law-breakers?

What shall I say of these save that they too stand in the sunlight, but with their backs to the sun?

They see only their shadows, and their shadows are their laws.

And what is the sun to them but a caster of shadows?

And what is it to acknowledge the laws but to stoop down and trace their shadows upon the earth?

But you who walk facing the sun, what images drawn on the earth can hold you?

You who travel with the wind, what weather-vane shall direct your course?

What man's law shall bind you if you break your yoke but upon no man's prison door?

What laws shall you fear if you dance but stumble against no man's iron chains?

And who is he that shall bring you to judgment if you tear off your garment yet leave it in no man's path?

People of Orphalese, you can muffle the drum, and you can loosen the strings of the lyre, but who shall command the skylark[6] not to sing?

热词天地

1.constancy ['kɒnstənsɪ] *n.* 不屈不挠，坚定不移
2.verily ['verɪlɪ] *adv.* 真实地，真正地
3.deem [di:m] *vt.* 认为，视为；主张，断定
4.vagrant ['veɪgrənt] *adj.* 流浪的；（思想）游移不定的
5.feast [fi:st] *n.* 盛会；宴会；宗教节日
6.skylark ['skaɪlɑ:k] *n.* 云雀

法律

于是一个律师说:"但是,我们的法律怎么样呢,夫子?"
他回答说:

你们喜欢立法,
却也更喜欢犯法。
如同那在海滨游戏的孩子,勤恳地建造了沙塔,然后又嘻笑地将它毁坏。
但是当你们建造沙塔的时候,海洋又送许多的沙土上来,
到你们毁坏那沙塔的时候,海洋又与你们一同哄笑。
真的,海洋常和天真的人一同哄笑。

可是对于那帮不以生命为海洋,不以人造的法律为沙塔的人,又当如何?
对于那以生命为岩石,以法律为可以随意刻雕的凿子的人,又当如何?
对于那憎恶跳舞者的跛人,又当如何?
对于那喜爱羁轭,却以小牛和林中的麋鹿为流离颠沛的人,又当如何?
对于自己不能蜕脱,却把一切蛇豸称为赤裸无耻的老蛇的人,又当如何?

对于那早赴婚筵,饱倦归来,却说"一切筵席都是违法,那些设筵的人都是犯法者"的人,又当如何?

对于这些人,除了说他们是站在日中以背向阳之外,我能说什么呢?
他们只看见自己的影子。他们的影子,就是他们的法律。
太阳对于他们,不只是一个射影者么?
承认法律,不就是佝偻着在地上寻迹阴影么?

你们只向着阳光行走的人,哪种地上的映影,能捉住你们呢?
你们这乘风遨游的人,哪种的风信旗能指示你们的路程呢?
如果你们不在任何人的囚室门前,敲碎你们的镣铐,哪种人造的法律能束缚你们么?
如果你们跳舞,却不撞击任何人的铁链,你们还怕什么法律呢?
如果你们撕脱你们的衣囊,却不丢弃在任何人的道上,有谁能把你带去受审呢?

阿法利斯的民众呵,你们纵能闷住鼓音,松了琴弦,但有谁能禁止云雀不高唱?

The Farewell

And now it was evening.

And Almitra the seeress said, "Blessed be this day and this place and your spirit that has spoken."

And he answered, Was it I who spoke? Was I not also a listener?

Then he descended[1] the steps of the Temple and all the people followed him. And he reached his ship and stood upon the deck.

And facing the people again, he raised his voice and said:

People of Orphalese, the wind bids me leave you.

Less hasty[2] am I than the wind, yet I must go.

We wanderers, ever seeking the lonelier way, begin no day where we have ended another day; and no sunrise finds us where sunset left us.

Even while the earth sleeps we travel.

We are the seeds of the tenacious[3] plant, and it is in our ripeness and our fullness of heart that we are given to the wind and are scattered.

Brief were my days among you, and briefer still the words I have spoken.

But should my voice fade in your ears, and my love vanish in your memory, then I will come again,

And with a richer heart and lips more yielding to the spirit will I speak.

Yea, I shall return with the tide,

And though death may hide me, and the greater silence enfold me, yet again will I seek your understanding.

And not in vain will I seek.

If aught I have said is truth, that truth shall reveal itself in a clearer voice, and in words more kin to your thoughts.

I go with the wind, people of Orphalese, but not down into emptiness;

And if this day is not a fulfillment of your needs and my love, then let it be a promise till another day.

Man's needs change, but not his love, nor his desire that his love should satisfy his needs.

Know therefore, that from the greater silence I shall return.

The mist that drifts away at dawn, leaving but dew in the fields, shall rise and gather into a cloud and then fall down in rain.

And not unlike the mist have I been.

In the stillness of the night I have walked in your streets, and my spirit has entered your houses,

And your heart-beats were in my heart, and your breath was upon my face, and I knew you all.

Ay, I knew your joy and your pain, and in your sleep your dreams were my dreams.

And oftentimes I was among you a lake among the mountains.

I mirrored the summits in you and the bending slopes, and even the passing flocks of your thoughts and your desires.

And to my silence came the laughter of your children in streams, and the longing of your youths in rivers.

And when they reached my depth the streams and the rivers ceased not yet to sing.

But sweeter still than laughter and greater than longing came to me.

It was the boundless in you;

The vast man in whom you are all but cells and sinews;

He in whose chant all your singing is but a soundless throbbing.

It is in the vast man that you are vast,

And in beholding him that I beheld you and loved you.

For what distances can love reach that are not in that vast sphere?

What visions, what expectations and what presumptions can outsoar that flight?

Like a giant oak tree covered with apple blossoms is the vast man in you.

His might binds you to the earth, his fragrance lifts you into space, and in his durability you are deathless.

You have been told that, even like a chain, you are as weak as your weakest link.

This is but half the truth.

You are also as strong as your strongest link.

To measure you by your smallest deed is to reckon the power of ocean by the frailty of its foam.

To judge you by your failures is to cast blame upon the seasons for their inconsistency.

Ay, you are like an ocean,

And though heavy-grounded ships await the tide upon your shores, yet, even like an ocean, you cannot hasten your tides.

And like the seasons you are also,

And though in your winter you deny your spring,

Yet spring, reposing within you, smiles in her drowsiness and is not offended.

Think not I say these things in order that you may say the one to the other, "He praised us well. He saw but the good in us."

I only speak to you in words of that which you yourselves know in thought.

And what is word knowledge but a shadow of wordless knowledge?

Your thoughts and my words are waves from a sealed memory that keeps records of our yesterdays,

And of the ancient days when the earth knew not us nor herself,

And of nights when earth was upwrought with confusion.

Wise men have come to you to give you of their wisdom. I came to take of your wisdom:

And behold I have found that which is greater than wisdom.

It is a flame spirit in you ever gathering more of itself,

While you, heedless of its expansion, bewail the withering of your days.

It is life in quest of life in bodies that fear the grave.
There are no graves here.
These mountains and plains are a cradle and a stepping-stone.
Whenever you pass by the field where you have laid your ancestors look well there-upon, and you shall see yourselves and your children dancing hand in hand.
Verily you often make merry without knowing.

Others have come to you to whom for golden promises make unto your faith you have given but riches and power and glory.
Less than a promise have I given, and yet more generous have you been to me.
You have given me my deeper thirsting after life.
Surely there is no greater gift to a man than that which turns all his aims into parching lips and all life into a fountain.

And in this lies my honor and my reward, —

That whenever I come to the fountain to drink I find the living water itself thirsty;

And it drinks me while I drink it.

Some of you have deemed me proud and over-shy to receive gifts.

Too proud indeed am I to receive wages, but not gifts.

And though I have eaten berries among the hills when you would have had me sit at your board,

And slept in the portico of the temple when you would gladly have sheltered me,

Yet was it not your loving mindfulness of my days and my nights that made food sweet to my mouth and girdled my sleep with visions?

For this I bless you most:

You give much and know not that you give at all.

Verily the kindness that gazes upon itself in a mirror turns to stone,

And a good deed that calls itself by tender names becomes the parent to a curse.

And some of you have called me aloof, and drunk with my own aloneness,

And you have said, "He holds council with the trees of the forest, but not with men.

He sits alone on hill-tops and looks down upon our city."

True it is that I have climbed the hills and walked in remote places.

How could I have seen you save from a great height or a great distance?

How can one be indeed near unless he be far?

And others among you called unto me, not in words, and they said,

"Stranger, stranger, lover of unreachable heights, why dwell you among the summits where eagles build their nests?

Why seek you the unattainable?

What storms would you trap in your net,

And what vaporous birds do you hunt in the sky?

Come and be one of us.

Descend and appease your hunger with our bread and quench your thirst with our wine."

In the solitude of their souls they said these things;

But were their solitude deeper they would have known that I sought but the secret of your joy and your pain,

And I hunted only your larger selves that walk the sky.

But the hunter was also the hunted:

For many of my arrows left my bow only to seek my own breast.

And the flier was also the creeper;

For when my wings were spread in the sun their shadow upon the earth was a turtle.

And I the believer was also the doubter;

For often have I put my finger in my own wound that I might have the greater belief in you and the greater knowledge of you.

And it is with this belief and this knowledge that I say,

You are not enclosed within your bodies, nor confined to houses or fields.

That which is you dwells above the mountain and roves with the wind.

It is not a thing that crawls into the sun for warmth or digs holes into darkness for safety,

But a thing free, a spirit that envelops the earth and moves in the ether.

If these be vague words, then seek not to clear them.

Vague and nebulous is the beginning of all things, but not their end,

And I fain would have you remember me as a beginning.

Life, and all that lives, is conceived in the mist and not in the crystal.

And who knows but a crystal is mist in decay?

This would I have you remember in remembering me:

That which seems most feeble and bewildered in you is the strongest and most determined.

Is it not your breath that has erected and hardened the structure of your bones?

And is it not a dream which none of you remember having dreamt that builded your city and fashioned all there is in it?

Could you but see the tides of that breath you would cease to see all else,

And if you could hear the whispering of the dream you would hear no other sound.

But you do not see, nor do you hear, and it is well.

The veil that clouds your eyes shall be lifted by the hands that wove it,

And the clay that fills your ears shall be pierced by those fingers that kneaded it.

And you shall see.

And you shall hear.

Yet you shall not deplore having known blindness, nor regret having been deaf.

For in that day you shall know the hidden purposes in all things,

And you shall bless darkness as you would bless light.

After saying these things he looked about him, and he saw the pilot of his ship standing by the helm[4] and gazing now at the full sails and now at the distance.

And he said:

Patient, overpatient, is the captain of my ship.

The wind blows, and restless are the sails;

Even the rudder begs direction;

Yet quietly my captain awaits my silence,

And these my mariners, who have heard the choir[5] of the greater sea, they too have heard me patiently.

Now they shall wait no longer.

I am ready.

The stream has reached the sea, and once more the great mother holds her son against her breast.

Fare you well, people of Orphalese.

This day has ended.

It is closing upon us even as the waterlily upon its own tomorrow.

What was given us here we shall keep,

And if it suffices not, then again must we come together and together stretch our hands unto the giver.

Forget not that I shall come back to you.

A little while, and my longing shall gather dust and foam for another body.

A little while, a moment of rest upon the wind, and another woman shall bear me.

Farewell to you and the youth I have spent with you.

It was but yesterday we met in a dream.

You have sung to me in my aloneness, and I of your longings have built a tower in the sky.

But now our sleep has fled and our dream is over, and it is no longer dawn.

The noontide[6] is upon us and our half waking has turned to fuller day, and we must part.

If in the twilight of memory we should meet once more, we shall speak again together and you shall sing to me a deeper song.

And if our hands should meet in another dream, we shall build another tower in the sky.

So saying he made a signal to the seamen, and straightway they weighed anchor and cast the ship loose from its moorings, and they moved eastward.

And a cry came from the people as from a single heart, and it rose into the dusk and was carried out over the sea like a great trumpeting.

Only Almitra was silent, gazing after the ship until it had vanished into the mist.

And when all the people were dispersed[7] she still stood alone upon the sea-wall, remembering in her heart his saying,

"A little while, a moment of rest upon the wind, and another woman shall bear me."

热词天地

1.descend [dɪ'send] v. 下来，下降；下斜
2.hasty ['heɪstɪ] adj. 仓促完成的；急忙的
3.tenacious [tə'neɪʃəs] adj. 顽强的；黏着力强的
4.helm [helm] n. 舵，舵柄；掌舵，掌管
5.choir ['kwaɪə(r)] n. 教堂的唱诗班；唱诗队
6.noontide ['nu:ntaɪd] n. 正午，白昼
7.disperse [dɪ'spɜːs] vt. & vi. （使）分散，（使）散开

言别

现在已是黄昏了。

于是那女预言者爱尔美差说:"愿这一日,这地方,与你讲说的心灵都蒙福佑。"

他回答说,说那话的是我么?我不也是一个听者么?

他走下殿阶,一切的人都跟着他,他上了船,站在舱面。

转面向着大众,他提高了声音说:

阿法利斯的民众呵,风命令我离开你们了。

我虽不像风那般地迅急,我也必须去了。

我们这些飘泊者,永远地寻求更寂寞的道路,我们不在安歇的时间地点起程,朝阳与落日也不在同一地方看见我们。

大地在睡眠中时,我们仍是行路。

我们是那坚牢植物的种子,在我们的心成熟丰满的时候,就交给大风纷纷吹散。

我在你们中间的日子是很短促的,而我所说的话是更短了。

但等到我的声音在你们的耳中模糊,我的爱在你们的记忆中消灭的时候,我要重来。

我要以更丰满的心,更受灵感的嘴唇说话。

是的,我要随着潮水归来,虽然死要遮蔽我,更大的沉默要包围我,我却仍要寻求你们的了解。

而且我这寻求不是徒然的。

假如我所说的都是真理,这真理要在更清澈的声音中,更明白的言语里显示出来。

阿法利斯的民众呵,我将与风同去,却不是坠入虚空;

假如这一天不是你们的需要和我的爱的满足,那就让这个算是一个应许,直到践言的一天。

人的需要会变换,但他的爱是不变的,他的"爱必满足需要"的愿望,也是不变的。

所以你要知道,我将在更大的沉默中归来。

那在晓光中消散,只留下露水的田间的烟雾,要上升凝聚在云中,化雨下降。

我也未尝不像这烟雾。

在夜的寂静中,我曾在你们的街市上行走,我的心魂曾进入你们的院宅。

你们的心搏曾在我的心中,你们的呼吸曾在我的脸上,我都认识你们。

是的,我知道你们的喜乐与哀痛。在你们的睡眠中,你们的梦就是我的梦。

我在你们中间常像山间的湖水。

我照见了你们的高峰与峭崖,以及你们思想和愿望的徘徊的云影。

你们孩子的欢笑,和你们的青年的想望,都溪泉似地流到我的寂静之中。

当它流入我心中深处的时候,这溪泉仍是不停地歌唱。

但还有比欢笑更甜柔,比想慕还伟大的东西流到我的心中。

那是你们身中的"无穷性";

你们在这"巨人"里面,都不过是血脉与筋腱,

在他的吟诵中,你们的歌音只不过是无声的颤动。

只因为在这巨人里,你们才伟大。

我因为关心他,才关心你们,怜爱你们。

因为若不是在这阔大的空间里,"爱"能达到多远呢?

有什么幻象、什么期望、什么臆断能够无碍地高翔呢?

在你们本性中的巨人,如同一株缘满苹花的大橡树。

他的神力把你缠系在地上,他的香气把你超升入高空,在他的"永存"之中,你永不死。

你们曾听说过,像一条锁链,你们是脆弱的链环中最脆弱的一环。

但这不完全是真的。你们也是坚牢的链环中最坚牢的一环。

用你最小的事功来衡量你,如同用柔弱的泡沫,来核计大海的威权。

用你的失败来论断你,就是怨责四季之常变。

是呵，你们是像大海。

那重载的船舶，停在你的岸边待潮。你们虽似大海，也不能催促你的潮水。

你们也像四季。

虽然在你们冬天的时候，你们拒绝了春日。

你们的春日，和你们一同静息，它在睡中微笑，并不怨嗔。

不要想我说这话是要使你们彼此说："他夸奖得好，他只看见我们的好处。"

我不过用言语说出你们意念中所知道的事情。

言语的知识不只是无言的知识的影子么？

你们的意念和我的言语，都是从封缄的记忆里来的波浪，这记忆是保存下来的我们的昨日。也是大地还不认识我们也不认识她自己，正在混沌中受造的太古的白日和黑夜的记录。

哲人们曾来过，将他们的智慧给你们。我来却是领取你们的智慧：

要知道我找到了比智慧更伟大的东西。

那就是你们心里愈聚愈旺的火焰似的心灵。

你却不关心它的发展，只哀悼你岁月的凋残。

那是生命在宇宙的大生命中寻求扩大，而躯壳却在恐惧坟墓。

这里没有坟墓。

　　这些山岭和平原只是摇篮和垫脚石，

　　无论何时你从祖宗坟墓上走过，你若留意，你就会看见你们自己和子女们在那里携手跳舞。

　　真的，你们常在不知晓中作乐。

　　别人曾来到这里，为了他们在你们信仰上的黄金般的应许，你们所付与的只是财富、权力与光荣。

　　我所给予的还不及应许，而你们待我却更慷慨。

　　你们将生命的更深的渴求给予了我。

　　真的，对那把一切目的变作枯唇，把一切生命变作泉水的人，没有比这个更大的礼物了。

　　这便是我的荣誉和报酬——

　　当我到泉边饮水的时候，我觉得那流水也在渴着；

　　我饮水的时候，水也饮我。

　　你们中有人责备我对于领受礼物上太狷傲、太羞怯了。

　　在领受劳金上我是太骄傲了，在领受礼物上却不如此。

　　虽然在你们请我赴席的时候，我却在山中采食浆果。

　　在你们款留我的时候，我却在寺院的廊下睡眠。

　　但岂不是你们对我的日夜的关怀，使我的饮食有味，使我的魂梦甜妙么？

为此我正要祝福你们：

"你们给予了许多，却不知道你们已经给与。

真的，'慈悲'自己看镜的时候，变成石像。

'善行'自赐嘉名的时候，变成了咒诅的根源。"

你们中有人说我高傲，与我自己的"孤独"对饮。

你们也说过："他和山林谈论却不同人说话。

他独自坐在山巅，俯视我们的城市。"

我确会攀登高山，孤行远地。

但除了在更高更远之处，我怎能看见你们呢？

除了相远之外，人们怎能相近呢？

还有人在沉默中对我呼唤，他们说："异乡人，异乡人，'至高'的爱慕者，为什么你住在那鹰鸟作巢的山峰上呢？

为什么你要追求那不能达到的事物呢？

在你的窝巢中，你要网罗甚样的风雨，

要捕取天空中哪一种虚幻的飞鸟呢？

加入我们罢。

你下来用我们的面包充饥，用我们的醇酒解渴罢。"

在他们灵魂的静默中，他们说了这些话；但是他们若再静默些，他们就知道我所要网罗的，只是你们的欢乐和哀痛的奥秘。

我所要捕取的，只是你们在天空中飞行的"大我"。

但是猎者也曾是猎品。

因为从我弓上射出的箭矢，有许多只是瞄向我自己的胸膛。

并且那飞翔者也曾是爬行者；

因为我的翅翼在日下展开的时候，在地上的影儿是一个龟鳖。

我是信仰者也曾是怀疑者；

因为我常常用手指抚触自己的伤痕，使我对你们有更大的信仰和认识。

凭着这信仰和认识，我说：

你们不是幽闭在躯壳之内，也不是禁锢在房舍与田野之中。

你们的"真我"是住在云间，与风同游。

你们不是在日中匍匐取暖，在黑暗里钻穴求安的一只动物，却是一件自由的物事，一个包涵大地在以太中运行的魂灵。

如果这是模棱的言语，就不必寻求把这些话弄明白。

模糊和混沌是万物的起始，却不是终结。

我愿意你们当我是个起始。

生命，与一切有生，都隐藏在烟雾里，不在水晶中。

谁知道水晶就是凝固的云雾呢？

在忆念我的时候，我愿你们记着这个：

你们心中最软弱、最迷乱的，就是那最坚强、最坚决的。

不是你的呼吸使你的骨骼竖立坚强么？

不是一个你觉得从未做过的梦，建造了你的城市，形成了城中的一切么？

你如能看见你呼吸的潮汐，你就看不见别的一切。

你如能听见那梦想的微语，你就听不见别的声音。

你看不见，也听不见，这却是好的。

那蒙在你眼上的轻纱，也要被包扎这纱的手揭去；

那塞在你耳中的泥土，也要被那填塞这泥土的手指戳穿。

你将要看见。

你将要听见。

你不为曾经失明而悲痛，你也不为曾经聋聩而悲悔。

因为在那时候,你要知道万物的潜隐的目的,你要祝福黑暗与同祝福光明一样。

他说完这些话,举目四顾,他看见他船上的舵工凭舵而立,凝视着那胀满的风帆,又望着无际的天末。

他说:

耐心的,我的船主是太耐心的了。

大风吹着,帆篷也烦燥了;连船舵也急要起程;

我的船主却静候着我说完话。

我的水手们,听见了那更大的海的啸歌,他们也耐心地听着我。

现在他们不能再等待了。

我预备好了。

山泉已流入大海,那伟大的母亲又把他的儿子抱在胸前。

别了,阿法利斯的民众呵。

这一天完结了。

他在我们心上闭合,如同一朵莲花在她自己的"明日"上合闭。

在这里所付与我们的,我们要保藏起来。

如果这还不够,我们还必须重聚,齐向那给予者伸手。

不要忘了我还要回到你们这里来。

一会儿的工夫,我的"愿望"又要聚些泥土,形成另一个躯壳。

一会儿的工夫,在风中休息片刻,另一个妇人又要孕怀着我,

我向你们,和我曾在你们中度过的青春告别了。

不过是昨天,我们曾在梦中相见。

在我的孤寂中,你们曾对我歌唱。因着你们的渴慕,我曾在空中建立了一座高塔。

但现在我们的睡眠已经飞走,我们的梦想已经过去,也不是破晓的时候了。

中天的日影正照着我们,我们的半醒已变成了完满的白日,我们必须分手了。

如果在记忆的朦胧中,我们再要会见,我们再在一起谈论,你们也要对我唱更深沉的歌曲。

如果在另一个梦中,我们要再握手,我们要在空中再筑一座高塔。

说着话,他向水手们挥手作势,他们立刻拔起锚儿,放开船儿,向东驶行。

从人民口里发出的同心的悲号,在尘沙中飞扬,在海面上奔越,如同号角的声响。

只有爱尔美差静默着,凝望着,直至那船渐渐消失在烟雾之中。

大众都星散了,她仍独自站在海岸上,在她的心中忆念着他所说的:

"一会儿的工夫,在风中休息片刻,另一个妇人又要孕怀着我。"

泪与笑

The Criminal

A young man of strong body, weakened by hunger, sat on the walker's portion[1] of the street stretching his hand toward all who passed, begging and repeating his hand toward all who passed, begging and repeating the sad song of his defeat in life, while suffering from hunger and from humiliation.

When night came, his lips and tongue were parched[2], while his hand was still as empty as his stomach.

He gathered himself and went out from the city, where he sat under a tree and wept bitterly[3]. Then he lifted his puzzled eyes to heaven while hunger was eating his inside, and he said, "Oh Lord, I went to the rich man and asked for employment, but he turned me away because of my shabbiness; I knocked at the school door, but was forbidden solace[4] because I was empty-handed; I sought any occupation that would give me bread, but all to no avail. In desperation I asked alms, but They worshippers saw me and said, 'He is strong and lazy, and he should not beg.'

"Oh Lord, it is Thy will that my mother gave birth unto me, and now the earth offers me back to You before the Ending."

His expression then changed. He arose and his eyes now glittered in determination. He fashioned a thick and heavy stick from the branch of the tree, and pointed it toward the city, shouting, "I asked for bread with all the strength of my voice, and was refused. Not I shall obtain it by the strength of my muscles! I asked for bread in the name of mercy and love, but humanity did not heed. I shall take it now in the name of evil!"

The passing years rendered the youth a robber, killer and destroyer of souls; he crushed all who opposed him; he amassed fabulous wealth with which he won himself over to those in power. He was admired by colleagues, envied by other thieves, and feared by the multitudes.

His riches and false position prevailed upon the Emir to appoint him deputy in that city—the sad process pursued by unwise governors. Thefts were then legalized; oppression was supported by authority; crushing of the weak became commonplace[5]; the throngs curried and praised.

Thus does the first touch of humanity's selfishness make criminals of the humble, and make killers of the sons of peace; thus does the early greed of humanity grow and strike back at humanity a thousand fold!

热词天地

1. portion ['pɔːʃn] *n.* 一部分；一份遗产（或赠与的财产）；嫁妆；分得的财产
2. parch [pɑːtʃ] *vt.* & *vi.* （使）焦干，（使）干透
3. bitterly ['bɪtəli] *adv.* 苦涩地；痛苦地；不痛快地；残酷地
4. solace ['sɒləs] *n.* 安慰，安慰物
5. commonplace ['kɒmənpleɪs] *adj.* 平凡的，陈腐的；平庸的，普通的

罪犯

一个有着强壮身躯的青年,却因饥饿而瘦弱不堪。他坐在人行道上,向路人伸出双手,祈求怜悯,一遍一遍重复着自己可怜的处境,诉说着饥饿和屈辱的痛苦。

当夜幕垂降,他已唇干舌燥,却仍饥肠辘辘,两手空空。

他站起来走到城外,在一棵大树下坐下来,放声痛哭。随后,他在泪眼朦胧中仰望天空,饥饿难耐地说道:"主啊,我曾到财主那里找活儿干,结果因为衣衫褴褛,被赶了出来;我曾叩过学校的大门,却因两手空空,被拒之门外;我只求一个能糊口的差事,却从未遂愿。最后,只能沿街乞讨。可是主啊,你的信徒们看见我却说:'这小子身强力壮,他怎么行乞!'

主啊,母亲依你的意志生下了我,但现在世道却要我在生命结束之前回到你的身畔。"

这时他的脸色突然大变,他站起来,眼中闪着决绝的光。他折下树枝做成一支又大又沉的木棒,指着城市大喊:"我尽力地乞求面包但被拒绝,现在我要用我的臂力去求生!我以仁爱之名乞讨面包,但人们从不留意。现在我将以邪恶之名去掠夺。"

几年过去了,年轻人已成为了一个劫匪、杀手和灵魂的毁灭者;他打压所有的反对者;他财富大增,并借此凌驾于权势之上。他被同行敬仰,被盗贼嫉妒,被百姓惧怕。

他的财富和虚伪之姿高涨,直到埃米尔王委派他当了执事——一个愚蠢总督的可悲安排。盗贼因此合法,压迫受到当局的支持;镇压弱者随处可见;人们只有屈从和赞美。

就这样,人们因自己的一己之私将一个可怜人造就成了罪犯,将一个和平之子变成了杀手;就这样,人类原始的欲望不断成长,并给人类以上千倍的反击。

Leave Me, My Blamer

Leave me, my blamer,
For the sake of the love
Which unites your soul with
That of your beloved one;
For the sake of that which
Joins spirit with mothers
Affection, and ties your
Heart with filial love. Go,
And leave me to my own
Weeping heart.
Let me sail in the ocean of
My dreams; Wait until Tomorrow
Comes, for tomorrow is free to
Do with me as he wishes. Your
Laying is naught but shadow

That walks with the spirit to
The tomb of abashment[1], and shows
Heard the cold, solid earth.
I have a little heart within me
And I like to bring him out of
His prison and carry him on the
Palm[2] of my hand to examine him
In depth and extract his secret.
Aim not your arrows at him, lest
He takes fright and vanish 'ere he
Pours the secrets blood as a
Sacrifice at the altar of his
Own faith, given him by Deity
When he fashioned him of love and beauty.
The sun is rising and the nightingale
Is singing, and the myrtle[3] is
Breathing its fragrance into space.

I want to free myself from the
Quilted slumber of wrong. Do not
Detain me, my blamer!
Cavil me not by mention of the
Lions of the forest or the
Snakes of the valley, for
Me soul knows no fear of earth and
Accepts no warning of evil before
Evil comes.
Advise me not, my blamer, for
Calamities have opened my heart and
Tears have cleanses my eyes, and
Errors have taught me the language
Of the hearts.
Talk not of banishment, for conscience
Is my judge and he will justify me
And protect me if I am innocent, and

Will deny me of life if I am a criminal.
Love's procession is moving;
Beauty is waving her banner;
Youth is sounding the trumpet of joy;
Disturb not my contrition, my blamer.
Let me walk, for the path is rich
With roses and mint, and the air
Is scented with cleanliness.
Relate not the tales of wealth and
Greatness, for my soul is rich
With bounty and great with God's glory.
Speak not of peoples and laws and
Kingdoms, for the whole earth is
My birthplace and all humans are
My brothers.
Go from me, for you are taking away
Life—giving repentance and bringing
Needless words.

热词天地

1. abashment [ə'bæʃmənt] *n.* 羞愧，害臊
2. palm [pɑ:m] *n.* 手掌，掌状物；（象征胜利的）棕榈叶，棕榈树
3. myrtle ['mɜ:tl] *n.* 桃金娘

for the sake of 为了

in depth 深入地，全面地

致非难者

非难我的人啊!请让我孤身一人!看在你心中怀有男女之爱,也不乏天伦之情,手足之感。你走开吧,留下我一个人,独守哭泣的心!

让我在自己的梦海中扬帆!耐心等待明日的降临,因为明日可以对我恣意妄为。你的非难不过是一种阴影,它与我的心灵同行,步向羞惭之墓,引向那人生——泥土一般刻板的人生。

我有一颗小小的心脏,我愿将他自牢中释放,将他捧于掌心细加端详,对它的奥秘深究到底。请别将你的弓箭对他瞄准,以免他恐惧万分,又躲藏进胸膛。他倾倒隐密之血正如将信仰作为祭坛上的祭品——这信仰本是主在用美与爱创造心时赋予他的。

这里,旭日正在升起,夜莺还在啼唱,桃金娘正在向大地吐露芬芳。我想离开谬误的柔软梦乡,非难我的人啊,请不要耽搁我。

不要用森林的狮子和山谷的毒蛇恐吓我。因为我的心从不知道恐惧,在灾难来临前,也不接受它的任何预警。

不要向我说教,我的非难者!因为灾难敞开了我的心怀,泪水擦亮了我的眼睛,而错误教会了我心灵的语言。

请别跟我谈论种种禁令!因为我的良心就是一个秉公而断的法官:我若无辜,他就将我庇护;我若有罪,他也会剥夺我的生活。

爱的队列在行进,美正在挥舞她的旗帜,青春奏着欢乐的进行曲。非难我的人,不要打扰我的忏悔!让我同他们一同前进!因为道路上铺满鲜花和香草,空气馨香而清新。

别再给我讲什么财富和伟大的传说!因为我的心灵因上帝的荣耀而如此富足和广大。

别再跟我谈论人民、法律和王国!因为整个地球都是我的祖国,世人都是我的兄弟。

离开我吧,因为你正在剥夺生命——只带来冗余和无用的言辞。

沙与沫（冰心 译）

1

It was but yesterday I thought myself a fragment[1] quivering[2] without rhythm in the sphere of life.

Now I know that I am the sphere, and all life in rhythmic fragments moves within me.

热词天地
1. fragment ['frægmənt] *n.* 碎片；片段，未完成的部分
2. quiver ['kwɪvə(r)] *vt.* & *vi.* 微颤，抖动

仅仅在昨天，我认为我自己只是一个碎片，
无韵律地在生命的穹苍中颤抖。
现在我晓得，我就是那穹苍，晓得生命是
在我里面有韵律地转动的碎片。

2

They say to me in their awakening, "You and the world you live in are but a grain of sand upon the infinite[1] shore of an infinite sea." And in my dream I say to them, "I am the infinite sea, and all worlds are but grains of sand upon my shore[2]."

热词天地

1. infinite ['ɪnfɪnət] *adj.* 无限的，无穷的；无数的
2. shore [ʃɔ:(r)] *n.* 岸；滨
   a grain of 粒；一点点，一些

　　他们在觉醒的时候对我说："你和你所居住的世界，只不过是无边海洋的无边沙岸上的一粒沙子。"

　　在梦里我对他们说："我就是那无边的海洋，大千世界只不过是我的沙岸上的沙粒。"

3

Seven times have I despised[1] my soul:

The first time when I saw her being Meek[2] that she might attain height.

The second time when I saw her Limping[3] before the crippled.

The third time when she was given to choose between the hard and the easy, and she chose the easy.

The fourth time when she committed a wrong, and comforted herself that others also commit wrong.

The fifth time when she forbore[4] for weakness, and attributed her patience to strength.

The sixth time when she despised the ugliness of a face, and knew not that it was one of her own masks.

And the seventh time when she sang a song of praise, and deemed it a virtue.

热词天地

1. despise [dɪ'spaɪz] *vt.* 鄙视，看不起
2. meek [miːk] *adj.* 温顺的；驯服的
3. limp [lɪmp] *vi.* 一瘸一拐地走；困难地航行
4. forbore [fɔː'bɔː(r)] *v.* ＜正＞(指为表示礼貌或耐心而)克制，容忍(forbear的过去式)
   attribute to 归因于，归咎于

曾有七次我鄙视了自己的灵魂：

第一次是在她可以上升而却谦让的时候。

第二次是我看见她在瘸者面前跛行的时候。

第三次是让她选择难易，而她选了易的时候。

第四次是她做错了事，却安慰自己说别人也同样做错了事。

第五次是她容忍了软弱，而把她的忍受称为坚强。

第六次是当她轻蔑一个丑恶的容颜的时候，却不知道那是她自己的面具之一。

第七次是当她唱一首颂歌的时候，自己相信这是一种美德。

4

Frogs may bellow louder than bulls, but they cannot drag the plough[1] in the field not turn the wheel of the winepress[2], and of their skins you cannot make shoes.

热词天地
1. plough [plaʊ] *n.* 耕作,耕地;犁
2. winepress ['waɪnpres] *n.* 葡萄榨汁器,葡萄榨汁机

青蛙也许会叫得比牛更响,但是它们不能在田里拉犁,也不会在酒坊里牵磨,它们的皮也做不出鞋来。

5

I have learned silence from the talkative,
toleration from the intolerant,
and kindness from the unkind;

yet strange, I am ungrateful to these teachers.

我已从健谈者那里学会了沉默，
从狭隘者那里学会了宽容，
从残忍者那里学会了仁爱。

但奇怪的是，对这些老师我心无感激。

6

You drink wine[1] that you may be Intoxicated[2]; and I drink that it may sober me from that other wine.

热词天地

1.wine [waɪn] *n.* 葡萄酒；果酒
2.intoxicate [ɪnˈtɒksɪkeɪt] *vt.* 使喝醉；使陶醉

你喝酒为的是求醉；我喝酒为的是要从别种的醉酒中清醒过来。

7

Only the dumb[1] envy the talkative[2].

热词天地

1.dumb [dʌm] *adj.* 哑的,无说话能力的
2.talkative ['tɔ:kətɪv] *adj.* 健谈的,多嘴的

只有哑巴才妒忌多嘴的人。

8

You cannot judge any man beyond your knowledge of him,
And how small is your knowledge.

你不能超过你的了解去判断一个人,
而你的了解是多么浅薄呵。

9

Once I spoke of the sea to a brook, and the brook thought me
But an imaginative exaggerator;

And once I spoke of a brook to the sea,
and the sea thought me but a depreciative defamer.

我曾对一条小溪谈到大海，
小溪认为我只是一个幻想的夸张者；

我也曾对大海谈到小溪，
大海认为我只是一个低估的诽谤者。

10

I would not listen to a conqueror preaching to the conquered.

The truly free man is he who bears the load of the bond slave Patiently.

我决不去听一个征服者对被征服的人的说教。
真正自由的人是忍耐地背起奴隶的负担的人。

11

A thousand years ago my neighbor said to me, "I hate life, for it is naught but a thing of pain."

And yesterday I passed by a cemetery and saw life dancing upon his grave.

千年以前，我的邻人对我说：
"我恨生命，因为它只是一件痛苦的东西。"

昨天我走过一座坟园，
我看见生命在他的坟上跳舞。